How to Become Meeting Royalty

First Edition
By Cliff Suttle

Published by Suttle Enterprises, LLC
Novi, Michigan

ISBN: 978-0-578-07763-5

Editing By Christine Eason and Marilyn Suttle

Printed in the US by InstantPublisher.com

To find out more about the author and other products and services turn to the last two pages of this book or visit their web-site at www.ExciteYourAudience.Com

Table of Contents

Chapter One
Meetings - Why Bother?

Meetings are the root of all evil - or, maybe evil is the root of all meetings, take your pick. At least, that's what I've been led to believe by the people who attend my workshops. If you were to sit in on the opening few minutes, you might believe this, too. The workshop quickly turns into a gripe session. "This is a waste of my time!", "That is the worst part of my job," or "Straight out yelling matches" are commonly heard bantered around. The feelings people share with me about meetings are frustration, boredom, and anger. Many people, even C-level executives, feel ineffective, useless, and bullied in meetings. This negative view of meetings is so prevalent, I'm surprised companies bother to have meetings at all. Why should companies bother with meetings when they result in so much hostility, lack of productivity, and frustration?

Truth is, like it or not, meetings are the best way to disseminate information, promote cooperation, and keep things moving, if they are done correctly. As I look out at the global business environment today, I see organizations that are being forced to change. The status quo isn't going to cut it anymore. Companies need to be leaner, cleaner, and more flexible. Products have to reach the market faster and with higher levels of quality and consistency.

Customers are demanding a better level of service. Gone are the days when ineffective meetings were tolerated. Therefore, gone are the days of running meetings as usual.

The problem I've seen with most meeting reform systems (and there are many out there), is that they focus on changing the structure of the meeting. While this might seem useful on the surface, it never achieves the desired meeting quality, and the gains rarely last. Before long, meetings go straight back into the muck, become bogged down and dirty. It's like fixing the forest without worrying about the trees. People are the core of any meeting, just as trees are the core of any forest. Create big, strong, healthy trees and the forest takes care of itself. Even just a few really strong trees can boost the heath of the entire forest. The same is true with meetings. It's difficult to get everyone on board with any change. Let's face it, people are change-resistant creatures. If you focus on changing the meeting agendas, diagrams, and planned meeting times, you've missed the mark. The forest isn't the problem, it's the trees.

One of the biggest flaws I see in other meeting reform systems is that they want to treat everyone in the meeting the same way. Everyone gets a timed turn, all ideas are written down, etc. etc. etc.

What a bunch of crap! Sorry, but that is the way I feel about it. The whole "one size fits all" idea just doesn't work for me.

This doesn't work in real life. Believe it or not, everyone in your meeting is different. It's like people have minds of their own or something! How annoying is that?

Each person has their own needs, desires, agenda, wants, hopes, dreams ... so on and so on. By treating everyone the same, you may hit the mark with some people and completely blow it with others. Some people need their hand held, other people hate that. Some people love all the nitty-gritty details, others are bored to tears by them. Some people love change, others hate, fear, and loath change.

Treating everyone the same is a recipe for disaster. Plus, other meeting reform systems require that everyone at the meeting be trained in the system. This doesn't work in real life, either. If you train everyone in your company on a meeting system, how long will it take before the system starts to erode? Due to attrition, layoffs, and firings, the staff changes over time. Unless you have an on-going meeting system initiative with every new employee, it won't take long until your costly investment and hard work in the meeting reform system will be for nothing. In addition, many of your meetings will be with clients, vendors, or others outside your organization who have never even heard of the meeting reform system you're using.

Even having meetings with the same structure every time is a disaster. Different companies have different cultures and biases. Managers will have personal styles. Departments often create a group personality unique to themselves. By forcing every meeting into a pattern, you can crush creativity, destroy motivation, and create the exact opposite of what you're trying to achieve.

That is why this book doesn't focus on changing the meeting, its focuses on changing you. If your meeting skills were to improve by twenty percent, then every meeting you attend would be positively affected. If your skills improve by fifty percent, you would be considered an essential player in any organization. If your skills improve one hundred percent, you would become invaluable. Notice we haven't changed the organization, we have just improved you.

How many people do you have to change in your company to affect every meeting you hold? In most corporations or organizations it would only be about ten percent of the work force. You can convince ten percent of your employees to buy into just about anything. Convincing ninety percent of your staff to change is usually a herculean task. This is why the techniques in this book are so unique and effective. Results are measured one person at a time. You don't need the entire corporation to change, just a chosen few. What you're about to learn will make changes easier to implement and maintain and have far reaching results. Plus, it's more dynamic in its processes.

Since you are taking time out of your busy schedule to read this book, we can assume that you are a leader or possess leadership potential. Interest in new ideas, and the open mindedness to accept or consider them, proves that you have a leadership attitude. Lead, and others will follow. So take this opportunity to pat yourself on the back, because you are the type of person every company needs. With your attitude and the techniques in this book, you will become "Meeting Royalty." Your mere presence in a meeting will change events for the better. Your regal abilities will make you rise above the crowd, allowing to you better determine the direction and fate of any meeting. Like a great monarch who guides a kingdom to greatness, you will be a positive influence on all meetings you attend.

In the chapters to come, you will be shown, in a practical way, how to identify the power structure of meetings, the motivational needs of the attendees, and how to keep control of your meetings while still achieving your personal and organizational goals. This book is not filled with mind numbing theory or impossible to implement processes; it contains simple to apply, pragmatic disciplines that work quickly and every time. The techniques explained in the book do take practice, but with a bit of commitment, you can become the king or queen of the ball. Think about it: no more frustration, anger, or pointless confrontations - just smooth sailing and effective outcomes. Not only will you improve your personal work environment, but you will affect the entire company or organization in a positive way.

The question on your mind right now should be, "will it really work?" Your time is valuable and reading and studying an entire book is an investment. Is this book worth the effort? Well, the proof is in the pudding, as they say. Let me share a quick story about the effectiveness of these techniques from personal experience.

I was called in to consult with a large union. They were having problems with their main corporate client, a Fortune 1000 company. Data was being lost between the union and the corporation that resulted in problems for union members. Benefits were not being tracked accurately. People were being un-enrolled from programs, and fees due were not being calculated correctly. Union members were complaining that their checks were "All messed up" almost on a daily basis. The union was taking the brunt of the customer service problems, but it was no picnic for the corporation, either. Time was going by without a solution, and the union and the corporation were pointing fingers at one another. In the middle of this battle was an unfortunate software vendor for the union and the IT department of the corporation.

After reviewing the data flow from input forms to the union member checks, it became clear to me that there was a fatal flaw in the data flow design. It was pretty easy for me to spot that there was no close in the data loop. Therefore, there was no verification to see if the original union data that was being exported to the corporation was stored or processed in a way that made it consistent with the original member information. My solution was simple: export the final data used to create corporate employee checks and compare it against the original member information in order to find and eliminate discrepancies. It might sound complex, but it really wasn't. This change to the data flow would allow both the union and the corporation to be proactive instead of reactive.

Have you ever noticed that sometimes when an answer is too simple, no one wants to believe it? Implementing this solution would take a day or two of manpower from both the union's software vendor and the corporation's IT department, which was a small price to pay to eliminate a major problem. They were paying me more money to find the solution than it was going to take to implement it. Despite all of this, getting people on board was a major battle. The union's software vendor thought it was a waste of time. The corporate IT department didn't want to admit they may have missed a potential data leak. The corporation stubbornly was supporting its system because it had "always worked before," and the union viewed it as entirely the fault of the corporation.

What a mess! Although there were many different agendas, there was only one problem. Caught in the middle of this quagmire were the poor union members with messed up checks. Finally, it was decided to have a big meeting with all parties involved to straighten out the problem. I was brought in as the hired gun that was going to "magically" make everything right, despite the fact that no one wanted to listen to me. The union was counting on me and the corporation was well aware of my presence.

When the big day arrived, the meeting was civil even though everyone was upset. The meeting was scheduled to last as long as it would take, but estimates were about three to four hours. For the first hour, I said nothing, not a word, not a peep. The corporate representatives kept looking at me expecting me to go on the war path. The software vendor, whom I had already had a confrontation with privately, was expecting me to blast them at any moment, blaming it all on them. Meanwhile the union representatives were perplexed. I'm sure they were thinking, "What are we paying this guy for if he is just going to sit there?"

While it seemed like I was being ineffectual, I was actually studying the dynamics of the group. I was identifying the key players, analyzing their motivational factors, and studying their meeting strategy techniques. I was making notes that appeared to others as if I were doodling. In the second hour, I started interjecting questions; not because I necessarily wanted the answers, but rather to see the way people on all sides would react. Would they get defensive? Would they triangulate others into their problem? Would they pass the buck, or point fingers? I made notes of this, too. Finally, I presented my solutions to the problem and watched as one group after the other chewed it up and spit it out. At no time did I try to defend my solution.

At about the 2-1/2 hour mark, the meeting started to wrap up. I'm sure the union was feeling as if they had wasted their money on me. It was at this point that I revealed the grand flaw in their thinking that pretty much unraveled everything they had done in the last 2-1/2 hours. I did this without pointing fingers or laying blame. As far as I was concerned, all they had accomplished in the first 2-1/2 hours was to realize (with a little prompting on my part) that they all had one thing in common: the problem. The real meeting started at this point.

In the next half hour, I reintroduced my solution, convinced the software vendor to commit to an implementation date, got the major corporate IT players to become my allies, and watched as the union staff began to smile. I walked out of that meeting with everything I wanted and made no enemies in the process. On the contrary, the different groups were looking forward to working with me again. Within three weeks of implementation, ninety percent of the data errors were eliminated and a plan was put in place to eliminate the rest. The union employees got their benefits straightened out, the union was happy, the software vendor quit getting complaint phone calls every day. Here was a win-win-win-win-win situation if I've have ever seen one.

This illustrates of how one person, armed with the right tools, can change a problem situation into a productive meeting. Often the solution to any problem is readily available if you can just get people to get out of their own way.

Now it's your turn. Ready for some new tools? Do you want to be the one that can turn a meeting around? Get ready, it's going to be an interesting ride.

Chapter Two
Understanding Personal Strategy
All the World's a Chess Game

In order to become "Meeting Royalty", you need to be able to identify the players quickly and accurately. Some people hate the word "players," but I've always thought that meetings should be fun, like a game, instead of hard, like work. Games have players, organizations have employees. Once the players have been evaluated, you can apply some easy rules to improve your dealings with them. This will cause them to buy into your ideas, bolster relationships, and limit confrontation. But, you can't identify the players without a program. You're about to discover how to identify and stratify the players in any meeting.

In this chapter, we will be studying the power structure of a meeting and its effect on the function of it. Some people think of a power structure as a bad thing, but nothing could be further from the truth. An organization chart is nothing more than a way for a company attempting to understand its power structure. All organizations need a power structure to survive. However, in a meeting, the organizational chart may not reflect the true power structure of the players in attendance. By gathering power structure information and learning your place within it, you will greatly improve your chances of creating a successful outcome for the organization.

As a teenager, I was a chess player. I could play as many as ten games at once against good players and win almost all of them. What took me years to realize was that I wasn't just playing a game, I was training myself to successfully navigate business meetings. Right from my first job out of college, I was considered a shrewd negotiator, but I was never conscious of why. It wasn't until years later, when I was sitting in a board of directors meeting, that it suddenly dawned on me: I was looking at a giant chess board. All the familiar pieces were there: queens, rooks, pawns. The same strategies were being used: mutual protection, forking, protective structures. Even the goals of the people in the meeting were the same as a chess game: consolidation of power.

It is not a coincidence that royals through the centuries have been taught how to play chess. It was mandatory learning for princes and princesses all across Europe. The Far East even had its own version of chess called "Go." Go was similar to chess in that it involved strategy and a consolation of power in order to win. At some point in the middle ages, the ruling class realized that training your mind in this way was an essential element in running a country.

Over a few years, I studied every meeting I attended and began to analyze it like a chess match. By taking what I had always secretly known in the back of my mind and making it a conscious thought process, soon whenever there was a problem, I was the guy they invited to the meeting. I want to share this revelation with you. We'll begin by looking at the power structure of a meeting. This section will be easier to understand if you know how to play chess, but knowing the game is not necessary. I will explain all of the important concepts in my metaphor as we proceed.

Here is your first chance to open your mind to a new concept - all meeting attendees are like chess pieces. In the game of chess there are six different classes of pieces: kings, queens, bishops, knights, rooks, and pawns. Each piece in the game has unique properties, advantages, and weaknesses. People in a meeting are the same way. By stratifying everyone as a chess piece, it's easy to decide how to respond to them and clearly keep their authority and influence in the forefront of your mind.

Among serious chess players, there is a way of determining the effective power of a piece by giving it a point value. This is an important thing to keep in mind while reading the rest of this chapter. Here are the point structures:

Pawns - 1 point
Knights - 3 points
Bishops - 3 points
Rooks - 5 points
Queen - 9 points
King - If you lose the king, you lose the game.

This is a great way to view a meeting. If someone at the meeting is functioning as a Queen, their backing for your idea is more valuable than a Knight and a Bishop combined. Chess players use this as a way of evaluating piece trades; this technique can be used in a similar fashion in meetings.

I am going to share the traits of each piece, how you can identify them, and how to best work with them in a meeting. Each of the following sections will be laid out in the following manner:

1) **Definition** - How this piece functions in the game of chess.

2) **Explanation** - How this relates to a person in a meeting.

3) **Identification** - How to spot this piece/person at a meeting.

4) **Management** - How to best deal with a person identified as this piece.

5) **Facilitation** - How to best function in a meeting if you are this piece.

It's important to keep in mind that people may function as different pieces from meeting to meeting. At a department staff meeting, the department head may be the King, but that same person could be a pawn at a board of directors' meeting. Therefore, it is important to re-evaluate everyone at every meeting.

Pawns - 1 point

1) **Definition** - A pawn is a very low value piece. It can only move forward and only one space at a time, or two spaces forward on its first move. It can only threaten two squares at once and is mainly used for support of other pieces. However, an interlocking collection of pawns can be used as a strong defensive structure. Pawns are expendable and worth trading with any other piece in the game.

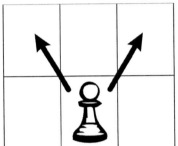

There is a common saying in popular culture: "send the pawns in first." This saying refers to a situation where you send in the less valuable assets so you can figure out your opponent's strategy before you commit the bulk of your forces.

2) **Explanation** - Pawns have no real authority in the organization that is significant enough to make any difference to the meeting. They also have little, if any, influence on the players of the meeting. They are usually only in meetings to give status reports in support of more powerful players, ideas, or projects. Some players will also let pawns present bad news or controversial ideas. This is also sometimes known in political circles as, "throwing them under the bus." Their individual vote counts for very little. However, just like the pawns in chess, if you have enough of them working together, they can protect and support each other. An example of this might be all the support staff in the department rallying together to remove the ban on employees parking close to the building.

3) **Identification** - Pawns are generally quiet at meetings and will only speak when called upon. They often sit near more powerful players. You will usually see them looking to more powerful players for support or instructions on meeting protocol. Pawns often know they are pawns and that they have little or no affect on the meeting's outcome. Since they aren't overly invested in the meeting's outcome, they can often appear bored or uncaring.

4) **Management** - Pawns are great for going first. Let them introduce facts and figures or give progress reports. They can be useful for keeping track of meetings or showing force in numbers. If there are pawns in your meeting, don't spend much time bringing them on board. Their vote counts for little, and often they don't really care anyway. For the most part, they can be ignored. But, if there are a lot of pawns all working together, this can turn into a strong mob. Be wary of this, since as a collection pawns are much more powerful pieces. A labor union works this way. A collection of pawns make good allies if they are on your side. If they stand against your ideas, using mob mentality works by convincing them to disagree with each other, thereby breaking up their protective structure.

5) **Facilitation** - If you are a pawn at the meeting, sit down and shut up. Perform the duties you came there to supply and let the more powerful pieces duke it out. Trying to over-extend your role is a good way to get your head chopped off.

Knights - 3 points

1) **Definition** - A knight is a sneaky piece because they don't attack in a straight line. Knights, also known as "horsies" to chess novices, move two squares in one direction and then proceed to move one more square at a ninety degree angle. Their unique mobility (they are the only piece in the

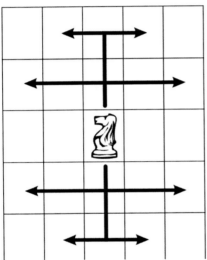

game like this) allows them to attack or defend other pieces in a stealthier way. The knight is always good at "forking" other pieces. "Forking" means to attack or defend multiple pieces at once. Especially on the attack, the knight's power play can be easily missed until they strike. The knight is good at threatening other pieces without being in danger itself.

2) **Explanation** - Like their namesake, people who are playing the knight's role at a meeting like to triangulate others into the discussion. They are good at forming alliances without looking like they are involved. They are also good at having other players fight their battles for them. Some people might call this sneaky, others strategic, but either way a knight is someone to keep your eye on. They love forming alliances outside the meeting and then blindsiding players at the meeting. The knight can be a

powerful ally or a dangerous foe.

3) **Identification** – Since they are hard to pin down, it can be hard to deal with the knights. You may think that you have their vote, then at the meeting they swing the other way. They are often quite political and can be self serving. I've learned to notice the long and telling glances between a knight and other players just before the player presents a new idea or negates someone else's suggestion. These looks are used to re-establish the alliance and signal to the other person that it's time to apply pressure. If you see someone who you suspect is a knight look at the ground when someone else is called upon to speak, this usually indicates a more devious agenda. In this case, the knight knows that an unpopular idea is about to be suggested and is trying to distance themselves from the source, which is often a source that they helped to create. Another tell-tale sign that you have a knight present are remarks like this after a new idea is suggested: "that's interesting, what do you think, Bob?" They already know what Bob thinks and are just trying to strengthen the argument. Knights rarely attack alone, so look for comments like, "I was talking to Susan and she agrees ..." or, "the other day at lunch, John and I thought it would be good ..." It's this willingness to triangulate other players into the argument that makes knights so dangerous.

4) **Management** - Dealing with knights can be beneficial or hazardous depending on whether they are supporting your position or attacking it. If you find yourself in a win-lose situation, a knight on the other team can be trouble. It is important to remember that fighting the knight gains you nothing. In fact, it could have the exact opposite

effect. Attacking or discrediting the knight directly may just cement the thinking of their allies. Remember that knights are very political and going up against one directly can be dangerous. Your best course of action against a knight is to attack their allies and try to win them over to your way of thinking. A knight standing alone is pretty useless, and they know it. If you sway a knight's allies to your cause, often the knight will switch sides too, which turns the knight from a foe into a friend. They don't like direct confrontation and, once friendless, will usually concede the argument. Knowing this about them, don't hold a grudge. If the knight wants to switch sides from antagonist to support, welcome them into your fold. The quote, "keep your friends close and your enemies closer," definitely holds true when dealing with knights.

If the knight is on your side, use that to your advantage. A knight is good at attracting and securing allies. Suggesting that the knight should talk to Susan at lunch about the plan is an effective way to utilize a friendly knight. By the end of lunch, your cause could have a new supporter and you didn't need to lift a finger. In a sales presentation, knights can work wonders before the meeting to secure support. They are good at making introductions to key players and setting the stage for your efforts. Often knights have no problem sharing or deferring credit- they would rather play from the shadows. By not hogging all the credit, they also take less of the blame should thing go poorly.

Warning: knights are political and can change sides quickly if they think they are on the losing team. You need to keep tabs on knights to assure that they remain in your camp. Remember, they are good at blind-siding people and you don't want to be the person who gets blindsided. Keep them in the loop and involve them in important decisions or processes. If they feel they are being left out, that's when trouble can start brewing.

5) **Facilitation** - There is nothing wrong with being a knight despite how it may sound. Knights can get things done quickly by building loyal support. If you want to be a knight, remember that you will be most successful if you start the process well before the meeting. You need to go into the meeting with your power structure already in place. This is a good role to play if you have limited authority within the organization, but still want to push your agenda. It's important to know that knights rarely get the credit. This works well for knights because it helps them develop loyal allies who have a higher need for recognition. Many highly successful CEOs play the role of the knight. A knight in the background is a powerful force for positive results. A knight in the foreground is probably just on their way to getting fired. Be sure to remember that a knight standing alone is easy to pick off, so keep your friends close.

Bishops - 3 points

1) **Definition** - The bishop is wonderful at creating defensive power structures. They cover a lot of the board and their intentions are easy to spot. Since they move on a diagonal, they are useful for supporting other pieces. A bishop's position can be greatly improved by the presence of pawns. Pawns and bishops both threaten squares on a diagonal, which makes them good at defending each other. Due to the value of the bishop, chess players will protect the piece whenever it is threatened. A bishop can only attack either black or white squares, but not both. Because of this, two bishops working together are much more valuable. One bishop can attack white squares while the other attacks black squares, which allows two bishops to cover the entire board.

2) **Explanation** - A bishop in a meeting brings influence to the group. They may or may not have any actual authority in the organization, but influence can often have greater impact than authority. Their opinions are sought out and their approval of ideas or direction is important. They are normally straight from the hip shooters, you know where they stand and they are not afraid to tell you what they think. They are well liked or respected within the organization and this gives them the confidence to stand their ground on any decision. A bishop can wield far more power than their status within the organization grants them. Examples of this would be: a past president of an organization, the genius from research and development, or the marketing guru with her finger on the pulse of your target customers.

3) **Identification** - People are naturally drawn to bishops. At a meeting, chairs around them will fill up quickly. Bishops can often be found in conversation with other powerful players before and after meetings. During the meeting, they are often asked for their opinions, even if it is not their field or department. When they are speaking, others in the room will give them their full attention. It's as if the curtains open and the spotlight shines on them. People will sit up straighter, grab a pencil to take notes, or their eyes will widen just a bit when the bishop is talking. Bishops are often highly spoken of, so notice who is being praised before the meeting in order to help identify one. If more than two people say that Carol is "amazing," there is a good chance that Carol is a bishop.

4) **Management** - Bishops make fantastic allies, but can be the kiss of death as an opponent. If a bishop agrees with your point of view, have a conversation with this person before the meeting. Let them comment on or add complimentary key components to your plan. If you cannot do this, ask them for their opinion during the meeting every chance you get. Others, seeing that the bishop is on your side, will flock to your cause. If possible, try and give the bishop credit for ideas or concepts. A happy bishop is a thing of beauty. They are accustomed to and comfortable with being the center of attention and often crave it.

On the other hand, a bishop who is opposed to your ideas can sometimes be impossible to overcome. Whatever you do, don't try to prove them wrong. Whenever anyone's opinions come under attack, they will often stick to their guns like glue. A bishop will call in their markers and use their influence on the others to circumvent all of your efforts. I have seen many a good plan go down in flames due to the work of one strong bishop. Once you have crossed paths with a bishop, it's a long way back. Instead, share credit whenever possible, bring them in on your plan, and always allow them to look good. You can change the mind of a bishop to your way of thinking if you're patient. Slow is the key word here. Don't be in a rush to get your way. Work with the bishops for as long as it takes. Bulldozing a bishop is a bad play and, with their allies, they can crush you.

5) **Facilitation** - Should you find yourself in the role of bishop, it can be a comfortable place to be. As a high-end consult, I often find myself in this situation without having to do anything to earn it. I walk in the room and wham, I'm a bishop. I have no real authority to make any decisions, but people hang on my every word and want my opinion on everything. Typically, becoming a bishop in any organization takes times. People have to learn to trust you and respect your point of view. People who think they are a bishop, and try to act like one when they are not, are just seen as egotistical or pushy.

As a bishop, use your power wisely. Don't jump to conclusions prematurely. Carefully weigh the evidence before you choose a side or path. Remember, others will follow your lead. If you jump the gun on your choice of action and later decide to reverse field, others may have made a home for themselves in the other school of thought. Now you will have to convince them that you were wrong then and you're right now. They may blindly follow you the first time based on your bishop status, but maybe not the second time. As a bishop you are welding a powerful weapon. It's important not to abuse your power and to hold back influence when not critically needed. Running around doing the bishop dance on every tiny issue will just dilute your influence.

The Rook - 5 points

1) **Definition** - The rook, sometimes known as a "castle," is a powerful piece. It can move vertically or horizontally as far as it wants. Rooks are typically protected by pawns for the early part of the game, but once out on the open board, rooks are a force to be reckoned with. Good at both defense and offense, rooks are used carefully by chess masters and not traded for other pieces unless it gains the player a distinct advantage in position or power structure. Only the queen (and of course, the king) is more valuable.

2) **Explanation** - Rooks at a meeting have authority in the organization. They weld budgets, resources, and/or decision making power. Managers, directors, and board members are all examples of rooks. Like their namesake, a rook is often protected by pawns, knights, and bishops that may be under their authority. They are uniquely different than bishops in that they have the power to make the decision.

3) **Identification** - Spotting a rook is pretty easy; often all you have to do is look at the company's organiza-

tional chart. Many rooks will sit at the back of the room in an unassuming location. They know they have the authority to override many decisions, so there is no need for them to jockey for position. They can often be quiet for lengthy periods of time while they gather information to make their decision. When a rook speaks, it is usually with confidence and authority. They didn't get to this position by accident, so assume they know how to take advantage of their power.

4) **Management** - Since a rook can make decisions based on their whims, it's important to keep them placated and to know their positions on the agenda and within the organization. Weeks of planning and preparation can be wiped out with the sweep of a rook's hand. Although not the ultimate decision maker, a rook's ability to control resources can put the kibosh on any plan if they have not been bought into the idea. Therefore, it is important to get them to buy in on any idea that will require the resources they have under their control. Even more powerful pieces (queens and kings) should keep this in mind. A slighted rook can reallocate resources is such a way as to slow the implementation of any plan to a crawl. As leaders, I'm sure you know that timeliness can be the difference between success and failure. Never assume that just because you're higher on the organization chart that you can control a rook's every action. Working with them to achieve a win-win situation whenever possible will be your best chance of success.

5) **Facilitation** - Functioning as a rook in a meeting can be fun and nerve raking all at the same time. You have the authority to assert your will, but as they say, "the buck

stops here." Going against the grain of popular opinion may leave you holding the bag for any decision. Should the decision turn out to be a bad one, you will be the scapegoat guaranteed. Also, stepping on a bishop with your authority can be costly to your own influence. Bishops have friends, and while you may get your way this time, you might be shooting yourself in the foot down the road.

Using your authority to step on a knight may create an evil ninja within your mists. Keep in mind that knights are political and often work their magic in the shadows.

Being in a position of authority also means responsibility. The buck really does stop here. Some days you need to use your authority to bring the hammer down and make the right choice, not the popular one. You didn't get to your position for nothing, you're a big boy/girl and you understand this. However, doing this over and over again will eventually make you unpopular. Now, I hear what you're saying: "it's not my job to be liked." That may be true, but bad rulers are often assassinated. Use your authority wisely, pick your battles, and use the authority hammer only when absolutely necessary. Align yourself with other rooks. Multiple rooks working together can be quite productive. Battles between rooks rarely end well. Find some common ground with them and work as a team.

Recruit bishops into your ranks whenever possible. They are great support players in your meetings and can bridge the gap between authority and influence. If you're lucky enough to be a rook with a bishop ally, you will be highly successful in meetings. Allying yourself with knights can be trouble since it could cause you to alienate other rooks. A knight can make moves leveraging your position without you even knowing what they are up to.

The Queen - 9 points

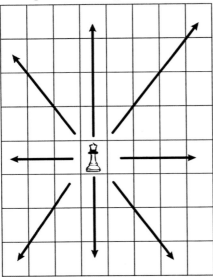

1) **Definition** - The queen is the most powerful piece in the game of chess. Able to move as far as she wants in all directions, queens can threaten, defend, and support other pieces all at the same time. Only a knight can directly threaten a queen without being in peril itself. When threatened, a good chess player will sacrifice any other piece (except for the king) to remove the queen from the board.

2) **Explanation** - Queens have a lot of authority and influence (think rook-bishop combination). They can cut across departmental or divisional lines to affect change in any part of the organization. They are used to using their power and have become accustomed to it. A vice-president is an example of a queen position. A queen cannot override every decision, but the king will rely on them heavily for advice.

3) **Identification** - It's pretty easy to identify a queen - they usually storm their way into a meeting. They ask "pin you to the wall" type questions, demand results, and call people on the carpet for poor performance. They often look like they know they are in charge, because,

well, they are. Expect them to sit in a commanding place, like the head of the table, and take control of the pace and direction of the meeting. Even rooks will acquiesce to their authority, both in action and mannerism. Queens are confident to a fault and this will be written all over their faces.

4) **Management** - Queens will dictate the relationship that you have with them. Since they can get their way on pretty much any issue, your only choice is to get them on your side. The queen's buy-in to your ideas is critical. Bishops and knights can be handy people to have on your side when dealing with an obstinate queen. Rooks will be less effective with queens since they are controlled by authority and queens are higher up in the pecking order.

Queens can weld their power in many different ways. They can be "bulldozer queens" and tell you the way it's going to be, or they can be "supportive queens", looking for ideas they want to support. A bulldozer queen can get a lot done fast, and in certain situations, it is exactly what an organization needs: someone who is not afraid to stand their ground and take control of a crisis situation. In a non-crisis situation, a bulldozer queen can cause talented individuals to leave the organization or even squash morale. A supportive queen can cut though the bickering, force opposing sides to work together, and bring cohesion to the group.

You normally need to get out of the way of a bulldozer queen. They will run you over if you are in their way. For a bishop, this may lower your influential standing and therefore, your effectiveness. As a knight, if you oppose a queen, you could find yourself standing alone, which is not a position a knight wants to be in. Knights need to follow the queen's lead. It's the penalty for being a knight. If you're a pawn, run for your life! Queens eat pawns.

A supportive queen is a stabilizing force in any meeting. Don't get in their way. Let them do their job and you might be invited to lunch with them now and again. It's always good to let a supportive queen know what motivates you. If they know what you want, and they like you, they are good at getting it for you.

5) **Facilitation** - So you have become the queen of the meeting, good for you. Now realize that the bigger they are, the harder they fall. We have all heard tales of powerful men and women being run out of town on a rail. You will be judged by your results. Poor results can cause a queen to tumble from power very quickly. Keep in mind that the meeting isn't about you, it's about results.

The best queens know when to be a bulldozing queen and when to be a supportive one. They will be comfortable in both roles and recognize when it is time to switch from one to the other. Queens that are stuck in a bulldozing or supportive role for too long will not be effective. A supportive queen who doesn't realize the need to be a bulldozer now and then is just waiting for a disaster to occur that will point out their lack of take-charge attitude. Someone who is always a bulldozer queen is headed for a mutiny or a mass exodus in the near future. By understanding your role in the organization as a leader, not a tyrant or a doormat, you can affect your meetings in powerful and profound ways. You get to set the tone of the meetings which can get the ball rolling in the right direction. If your meetings are not as successful as you'd like them to be, look no further for people to blame than yourself.

The King - The Game

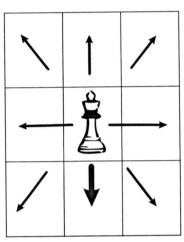

1) **Definition** - Although in the game of chess the King has no power value points, it still is the most important piece on the board. The reason for this is that if your opponent threatens the King and the King has nowhere to retreat, that is known as Checkmate and the game is over. You lose. The King can only move one space in any direction, so in terms of abilities a King isn't much more powerful than a couple of pawns, but players will sacrifice any piece, even the queen, to protect the King. Lose the King and you lose the game.

2) **Explanation** - In many meetings there will be a King. Sometimes the King can be represented at a meeting even when they are not physically present. Their wishes and desires are more important than any other factor at the meeting. Examples of Kings in business might be the CEO, Chairman of the Board, Angel Investor, or Head of Operations. Anyone who wields absolute power over the final decision of the meeting is the King. Everyone at the meeting understands the power they wield and will do everything they can to impress them. Once the King has made a decision, others will flock to protect the King's decree.

3) **Identification** - If you can't identify the King, you shouldn't be in the business world. If you enter any meeting without knowing who the ultimate decision maker is, that is a real problem. Always learn this information. Usually it's as simple as just asking someone.

4) **Management** - There are two types of Kings: internal and external. Most kings can bounce between the two types, so it's important to track where they are at the moment.

Internal Kings believe that they are right in all things. Their decisions are law and they will wield they mighty position to get what they want. An external King is looking for a group consensus. They surround themselves with smart people and listen to what they have to say. Often, they will pass decision making responsibility to queens or rooks, allowing them to take control of the meeting and the final decision.

An internal king will make the final decisions in all things. The decisions may not always seem logical because the king may or may not be sharing all the information they are using to decide the issue.

Dealing with a king can be difficult. You will always be straddling the fine line between doing what you believe is right and doing what the king wants. As a consultant, kings have made my life easy or have been a nightmare. I have been in situations where I know the company is on the path to hell, but that's the way the King wants it. I have had to sit and watch as the company sinks with little

I can do to change the course.

In one case I was unfortunate to be a part of, a consultant who conned his way into the company and whose only claim to fame was running one failed business, implanted himself as king. He was an internal king and didn't listen to anyone else. I, functioning as a bishop, worked with multiple engineering departments, listened to their needs and desires, and worked up a plan for a brand new engineering change tracking system. It was going to be revolutionary and all of the engineering department heads (rooks) were fully on board. With the stroke of a pen, the king wiped out the plan because it wasn't what his failed company had done and I was instructed to make a disaster of a software system that was never implemented because no liked it or was willing to buy into it. Obviously the king didn't know that you have to get the rooks on board to be successful.

Hmmmmm ... oh well, sometimes that's the way life works sometimes. The best I could do in this situation was collect our consulting fees, realize that when the system failed the king would hang my company on the hook with the blame (which he did), and just watch as the king moved onto the next bad decision. In time, with profits sagging, the king was removed from his throne, as bad kings often are. It can be nearly impossible to budge a stubborn king. History has been full of such situations. In Nazi Germany, Hitler's generals knew he was making bad decisions, but they were too afraid to do anything about it. Fortunately for the world, Hitler's internal king style made it easier for the allies to win the war. Many of his decisions sent troops to their deaths with no real gains in the process.

Dealing with someone who is always an internal king can be frustrating, if not outright maddening. The important thing is to keep your cool. You will always be more effective in meetings if you can stay calm and relaxed. Even when under fire, the calm head will be better off. Repeated poor performance by a king should be the sign that it is time for you to move on.

If you are dealing with an external King, the situation is much different. Convince them that you are someone worth listening to and you win the game. A king may have multiple queens hovering around them. These queens can be the key to reaching the mind and heart of the king. The king more than likely put the queens in power in the first place and probably trusts their input and decision making abilities. Allying with the queens and bishops is your best way to influence the King. Never fork the king with a knight or the term "off with your head!" may come into play.

Keep in mind that alienating the rooks while gaining the king's approval is a bad idea. You might get the decision you want, but implementing the decision may be difficult. Make sure you bring the rooks along for the ride. They will appreciate your confidence in them and this will increase your influence within the entire organization.

5) **Facilitation** - So you're the king. Good for you, now don't blow it. Internal kings who make good decisions can quickly achieve results. Their instant decisions and quick turns of direction can really make a company soar ... for a while. Internal kings can ultimately start thinking they can do no wrong, especially when they have a string

of good decisions behind them. They can get into trouble if they stop listening to their supporting players. Internal kings will often drive away the talent in their organization who made them successful in the first place and ultimately surround themselves with "yes" people. This results in poor decisions that are implemented without ever being challenged. This can cause a quick demise for a department, company, or organization.

A purely external king can be just as ineffective. Endless meetings and planning can drag a company down as easily as poor decisions can, it just takes longer. The ability to gather information, quickly analyze, and make definitive decisions is the trademark of all good kings. You need to trust your supporting players or replace them. Make sure your trust in queens is deserved and listen to your bishops since they often have their fingers on the pulse of the company.

The term "it's lonely at the top" is true. Sometimes you will have to make the unpopular decision. If you can't do this, you shouldn't be king. The ability to switch from external to internal when the time comes is important. General George S. Patton, one of the greatest American generals of all time, said: "A good plan today is better than a great plan tomorrow."

Chapter Three
Game Strategy

Now that we have a common set of power structure definitions to work with, the next step is understanding the game. Just learning how the pieces move does not make you a good chess player. Master chess players have learned the secret strategies that allows them to win more than they lose. There are strategies like this in business meetings, too. In this chapter, we will discuss the pinnacles and pitfalls of navigating a meeting. Remember that just because you are approaching meetings as a game, that doesn't mean there has to be a loser. The win-win scenario is always the desired outcome, although it's not always possible. It's important to remember that "Meeting Royalty" will get what they want out of a meeting, but the truly smart royals will work to make sure as many people as possible get what they want, too. The following strategies are just tools; how you use them is up to you.

Thinking Ahead - The Reaction Tree

In the game of chess, as in business, the person who is thinking two or three moves ahead will always win over the person who is reacting to whatever comes at them. Although this seems obviously true to anyone with half a brain, I can't count how many times I have gained the upper hand in a meeting just by anticipating the reactions of others. If I had to just pulled a number out of the air with only vast personal experience to back it up, I would say that 90% of people come into meetings totally unprepared for what they may have to face.

I find it funny when these people feel "blindsided" by the events that transpire. "Wow, I didn't see that coming," or, "that came totally out of the blue," or, "I wish someone had warned me," are common comments I hear after a particularly difficult meeting. It doesn't have to be this way. If you hear yourself utter any of these phrases after a meeting, stop, think, and decide if you were blindsided or if you just weren't prepared. If you're honest with yourself, you might be surprised at how often you discover that it was your fault. There is a funny anti-motivational quote I like: "All your failures have one thing in common: you." It is so much easier to change yourself than it is to change the world.

You need to think about how people will respond to your proposals. This anticipation can make all the difference in creating a positive outcome. Now, go one step further and decide how you will respond based on their reactions. The farther out you can look, the more influential you will be. This will improve the odds of producing a positive result from any meeting. Let's look at an example.

You have come to the conclusion that, in order to achieve company goals, the marketing budget should be increased by fifteen percent. You plan to present the idea at tomorrow's meeting. Before the meeting, you can create a "Reaction Tree" that looks something like this:

Present 15% increase in marketing budget

Reaction 1) Favorable reaction - people in general like the idea.

> **Your Action** - present an implementation plan and call for an immediate vote on the budget request.

Reaction 2) Mixed reaction - about a fifty-fifty split on whether people like it or not.

> **Your Action** - start a discussion aimed at finding out where people stand on the issue. Once you gather this information, call for the issue to be tabled and set another date to discuss it. This will give you time to enlist allies to your proposal before the next meeting based on the information you gathered.

Reaction 3) Hostile reaction - people think it's the worst idea since building Pompeii next to a volcano.

> **Your Action** – Quietly and objectively listen to people rant about how terrible the idea is. Form a clear picture of what the objections are and which chess pieces are making them. Move onto the next agenda item without complaint or argument, but get on the agenda for the next meeting without revealing the topic. Between meetings, rework the plan while taking the objections into account. Work on the bishops to get them on your side and see if they can influence the Queen. Ask the King to lunch and carefully discuss his objections. Create a new reaction tree for the next meeting.

This is a simplified version of the decision tree I would make before a meeting, but it presents the basic idea. By having your plans laid out in advance, you can react quickly to any situation and remain calm, even under fire. People will normally lose their cool when events are unexpected. The expected events rarely rattle us. Being known as someone who is cool under fire will go a long way in increasing your influence and credibility.

The second advantage to having a reaction tree prepared is that it allows you to set the pace of the meeting. One of my strategies when I played chess was to play the opponent's pieces in my mind, consider what all their best moves would be, and then create a reaction to them. This allowed me to wait, wait, wait for their move and then - POW! - surprise them with my move right away. This would often rattle my opponents and keep them on the defensive while constantly scrambling to keep up with me. The same thing holds true in meetings. If you are always ready for the next step in your agenda, you can react before anyone can put blocks in your way or have time to gather forces against your ideas. Remember that 90% of people do not think this way, so this will give you a definite edge.

Let's look at another example. You are making a sales presentation to the board of directors of a manufacturing company with a thousand employees. There is no king, but there are two queens. One is an expert on operations and the other is an expert on finance. Your presentation is about how to retool all the equipment to meet a higher standard. It is a large investment of capital goods. Here is a more complex decision tree:

Make opening presentation based on the generalized advantages of your proposal.

Reaction 1) They're impressed. Both queens seem excited.

> **Your Action** - Continue presentation with case study of performance.

Reaction 2) The operations queen is impressed, but the budget queen is skeptical.

> **Your Action** - Continue presentation with case study on cost saving.

Reaction 3) The budget queen is impressed, but the operations queen is skeptical.

> **Your Action** - Continue presentation with case study on cost saving and cement the backing of the budget queen. With the budget queen on your side, convince operations queen to talk about misgivings. Address the issues you can and set up a personal meeting with the operations queen and a technical specialist as soon as possible.

Reaction 4) They are both unimpressed.

> **Your Action** - Change tactics. Ask what they like and dislike about their current equipment. Let them talk as long as they want. Afterwards, allow them to describe their dream equipment. As they mention features that your products have, casually point that out. Look for knights and bishops on the rest of the board to help bolster your best product features.

This is a good opening game plan, but what if we take it a step further? The farther you think in advance, the more successful you'll be. Here is a piece of an example of how reaction 1 from the reaction tree above, could become a little more detailed:

1) Both queens are impressed.

    A) Presentation continues cost savings case study.

        I) Case study well received by both queens.

            i) Set up a time for shop floor evaluation and discuss specifications of final quote.

        II) Case study connected with operations queen only

            i) Invite operations queen and guest to a tour of your factory.

            ii) Set up a time to speak with the budget queen in private.

        III) Case study connected with budget queen only.

            i) Invite operations queen and supporting bishops and knights to lunch. This will allow you to separate their complaints from the rest of the group.

During my two day trainings about how to become "Meeting Royalty," this is often the point where people start to complain about how much work this is. My response is usually, "Really? You're presenting a seven figure proposal and you're worried about a little prep time?" This is where you separate the men from the boys or the women from the girls. Who wants to step up and play? The better question is: who wants to step up and sell a seven figure contract? If a little hard work scares you, then this is certainly not the book for you.

In Chapter 1, I talked about how 90% of people in meetings are asleep at the wheel. Well, like anything else, it takes a little work to be in the top 10% of anything. Are you the top 10%? The top 10% of your industry, the top 10% of your company, the top 10% of wage earners? Do you want to be? For the rest of the book, every time you think, "this is too much work," instead say: "I'm satisfied with being in the bottom 90%." If you're satisfied, great, the world only needs so many chiefs. If you're not satisfied with being in the bottom 90%, keep reading.

The main concept you need to take away from this chapter is: **don't think, outthink**. Meetings are a chess game. The player who outthinks their opponents will improve their position. By constantly having a plan, by always being ready with the next step, you will be miles ahead of anyone who is simply reacting. Imagine playing a football game where all you ever did was react. You had no plan, no strategy, and no plays. A team with smaller, slower, and weaker players could easily beat you if they had a good coach. You don't always need to have the best team to win the game. A better plan can go a long way. In a meeting, the players with the best plan will come out on top more often than not.

Holding Back

One of the worst things you can do in a meeting is start with your strongest ideas, points, or persuasive arguments. I see this mistake made so often that it scares me. People are so excited about their ideas that they rush to put them on the table. The problem with doing this, is that many (if not all) meetings have at least one naysayer. These are people who don't look for solutions - they look for problems. By presenting your best ideas up front, you give them plenty of time to formulate dozens of arguments as to why your idea will bomb. You also give them ample time to influence everyone else at the meeting. By the time the meeting is over, you could have quite a hole to climb out of.

Instead, let the pawns go in first. That's what pawns are for. Start with status updates, budget reports, other people's ideas, or anything else that will allow some time to study the traits and tactics of the other players. Have you ever been to a world title boxing match? The first few rounds are normally pretty boring. The boxers are usually just dancing around and don't throw very many punches. The boxers are feeling each other out, evaluating strengths, looking for weaknesses, and formulating a plan. This is exactly what I'm talking about. Now and then, a boxer will rush in and start mixing it up right away, but the vast majority of those types get themselves knocked out early.

Back in the 90's, one of my companies sold CAD (Computer Aided Design) software. The best attribute of the system we sold was that it was fast! With this system, there wasn't a lot of sitting around waiting for the screen to redraw. It was about 16 times faster than its nearest competitor. For its time, this was important because computers weren't very fast yet. Although it was an amazing feature, I never started a presentation with that information. I always began by showing off the standard features that you would expect from any CAD system. As I evaluated the people in the room, I was able to pick and choose who to focus on when presenting new features that were unique to the product. Near the end of the meeting, I would hit them with the withheld tidbit: the system's speed. That always made a big impact and left little, if any, time for anyone to dispute or downplay the effect of this product's advantage. This definitely gave me an edge and I sold a lot of software.

Let's look at this strategy in a win-win scenario. Let's say we are in union negotiations. Many people look at this as a win-lose situation, but in fact both sides benefit from a contract that works for the best interest of the company. If the company succeeds, everyone benefits. For the sake of this example, let's put you in the position of management. Over the last year, management has been working hard to secure a new source of health care that will be cheaper for the employees and offer better prescription benefits. It's your ace in the hole to help make the employees happy. The employees want a 10% raise in pay, something that would make the company highly unprofitable, and therefore is not an acceptable option. If you put the new health care option on the table right away, the union may be happy, but I can almost guarantee you that by the end of negotiations that perk will be all but forgotten.

The better strategy here is to wait and hold your ace for later. After some time at the bargaining table, you have worked on the pay raise until you are only 1% apart from each other. Now you play the big card and talk about the new heath care plan. Suddenly, management is starting to look like the heroes. The new attitude spreads into the rest of the negotiations and soon the contract is signed. The employees feel like they got a fair deal, the stock holders are happy, and management smells like a rose. A win-win situation. If the new heath care option had been presented first, you'd still be there bickering over a quarter of a one percent raise.

How do you know how to proceed? In concept, this is pretty easy, but it will take practice to master. The basic process is to release information or concepts when you have a good idea of how it will be received. In our fictitious example above, let's say that during negotiations you had noticed that two of the bishops mentioned health care more than once. The queen isn't worried about health care, only about getting a bigger raise for the union members. The queen asks the bishops for their opinions quite often. There is also a quiet rook who seems to completely hate management altogether, but she is forked by a knight with the queen. If the queen goes along, the knight will be sure that the rook comes along for the ride.

It is quite clear that the two bishops will be happy with the new health care arrangements. Therefore, you need to watch them to see when they are about to compromise on the raise amount. When you see that, you know it's time to play the big card and focus your attention mainly on the two bishops when you do. You have calculated that the bishops will love the new proposal, the queen won't be very impressed, and the rook will hate you no matter what you do. Once the bishops are excited, play to them and let bishops do what bishops do. They will soon influence the queen, who will start to bend on the raise. Once the knight sees the queen start to sway, the knight will play the support role with the rook and before you know it, the entire team is on board. Everybody wins!

Let's play out another example. The king has informed you that due to a highly profitable quarter, you have more budget than expected. You are mediating between two camps that are vying for the same budget. Two rooks have an idea for a new product and they want the monies for R&D. You have enough room in the budget to completely fund only one project and still have a little left over, but not enough to fund the second project. It's this surplus information that we are going to hold back sharing for now. The heads of both camps are powerful rooks in the organization. Even though you are the queen at this party, you know from experience that ticking off either rook will have repercussions.

I know that in a perfect world, the two sides would work together and harmoniously come to a decision that is best for the future of the company. Let's join our fairy friends and ride some unicorns all the way to the candy mountains because both of these are just about as likely to happen. Am I right?

Both sides want their project funded so they can produce the next big thing for the company and be the hero. This is the motivation the rooks are bringing to the meeting with them. As the queen, you could just come down and squash one side or the other and get things moving, but is this really the best way? You can just imagine the problems the rook who was squashed can cause without you even knowing it.

You already have a good idea of which product

would be best to pursue based on your personal experience and marketing studies you've read, but now you just need to get the rooks on board.

Your strategy should be to share the marketing information with both rooks and lead them both to your decision. Don't tell them the decision first, just let them start doing the thinking for themselves. At some point, the camp that supports product A will begin to get excited when they realize which way the wind is blowing. Camp B may start to get desperate and really pick up the fight for their point of view. It's important to listen to these arguments for two reasons. First, the rook will feel heard and second, you might just find out some new information that will make you rethink your choice. For the sake of argument, let's say that after rook B is talked out, you still want product A. You inform the rooks of your decision. Rook A is excited. Rook B is dejected and unmotivated.

Finally, you send Rook A on his ways to get things moving. Then, alone with rook B, you inform him about the additional monies in the budget and ask him to draft up some new ideas that could work within the more limited budget.

Is Rook B totally happy? No, but hey, that's the way the world works sometimes. However, you have tossed Rook B a bone to chew on and are keeping him too busy to worry about it. If you had mentioned the new budget in the beginning, Rook A would have felt cheated that he didn't get the additional funds, and Rook B wouldn't have felt any better about things either.

In the last two examples I have combined the concept of holding back with the concept of a reaction tree. During our "Meeting Royalty" training sessions, I sometimes hear complaints about how these are manipulative tactics. The truth is ... they can be. I mentioned in Chapter 1 that I am simply giving you the tools - what you do with them is your decision. In the two examples above, the tools were used to improve the results and make everyone happy with the final decision. Can these tactics be used to squash people? Yes, they can, if that's what you choose. I wouldn't choose that, but a hammer can be used to build or destroy a house.

I'm a big fan of history. I love little known facts about the past that can teach us all something today. Did you know that Winston Churchill (the famous leader of England during World War II) had very few bodyguards? I found this interesting, because Hitler had thousands of bodyguards and his enemies still managed to almost blow him up with a bomb. I'm too young to have met either of these historic figures, but I'm pretty sure they were both good at getting what they wanted in meetings. However, their eventual results from these meetings were quite different - not only for them, but for the world. Churchill used meeting tactics to bring people together. Hitler did not.

How you use these tools is your decision. Choose wisely.

Chapter Four
Something Smells Fishy
Motivational Factors

A t this point we are going to put away the chess pieces for awhile and focus on a new analogy, but don't worry, our chess playing friends will return later in the book. In the next few chapters we'll study personality trends and how to take advantage of them in meetings. This is my number one trick, so pay special attention. There are many different systems on the market that study personality types. You may already be familiar with some these systems: DISC, Predicative Index, Myers-Briggs, Psychogeometrics, etc. These systems are quite accurate in their ability to predict how someone will respond in a certain situation. Personality typing is a social science that began in earnest in the 1960's with the advent of modern psychiatry. My first introduction into this study was when I read the book "Please Understand Me," by David Keirsey and Marilyn Bates. I was fascinated by the entire subject. Along the way, I found that the systems that had been developed didn't really meet my personal needs as a meeting expert, so I really didn't use them. Instead I developed my own simplified system.

Personality classification systems can be quite useful for hiring and for project resource allocation. The problem I found with most of these systems was in their application in meetings. They were just too details to apply quickly and effectively on the fly. When you enter a meeting with relative strangers, you don't have long to analyze and determine your best approach for each person. Within ten minutes of the start of the meeting, you'd better have a good idea of what makes everyone tick or you'll be flying blind. Personality classification systems usually involve lengthy tests containing forty or more questions. You can't make the attendees of a meeting take one of these tests. Can you imagine walking up to a queen and demanding they take a sixty question test before you start a meeting? That meeting would be off to a poor start and the queen would be preparing to stomp you flat.

This is why I have developed my own simplified system. I only focus on "Motivational Factors," and I have pared those down to only four types. In a meeting, it is pretty much impossible to break down someone's personality into sixteen or more categories, like many personality classification systems do. Through much trial and error, I have found that four distinctive groups are plenty to identify and track during a meeting. My definition of a motivational factor is: the type of activities, information, or approaches that someone would find interesting or appealing. I'm looking for what will light them up. In a meeting, I can use motivational factors to increase the chances that someone will like my ideas or support my cause. Often, it's as easy as rewording an explanation that will make or break the deal. By changing my presentation on the fly to best suit the ears of the person I most want to influence, I take a large step forward in becoming "Meeting Royalty". Therefore, I highly recommend that you read the next few chapters multiple times, and reread it again at least every two months until the concepts become second nature to you. Yes, it's that important. No matter what type of meeting you're in, this can be a powerful force for swaying public opinion.

Because pictures and concepts are easier to remember than words, I have related my four motivational types to sea creatures. This metaphor works extremely well to help cement the concepts in your mind. My four fishy friends are; Sharks, Dolphins, Octopi, and Crabs. Let's start our understanding of these four motivational types by looking at the characteristics of their representative sea creatures.

Sharks

Sharks are single minded predators. They swim until they find a fish, then they stalk the fish, kill the fish, and eat the fish. They are nature's perfect task-driven animal. They are so well suited to their environment that they have remained relatively unchanged for two-hundred and fifty million years. Powerful and undaunted, the shark is the master of his domain. Their ability to stay laser focused on their prey has made them the most feared creature in the sea. Sleek and fast, they rarely waste energy on useless motions and every action they take has a purpose. Sharks have many unique and unusual senses such as motion and magnetic sensory organs in their noses and mouths. They navigate the waters in a 3D experience that humans can only imagine. Their dominating presence commands attention from all creatures large and small. They have been spotted hunting in packs, but prefer to hunt alone and once they strike, their prey has little chance of survival.

Dolphins

Dolphins are fun loving
and playful creatures who take
great joy in everything they do,
from courtship to hunting.
They live in closely knit pods
of forty to fifty individuals and rarely swim alone.
Intelligent, loyal, and inquisitive, the dolphin is
unique among sea creatures in their ability to interact not
only with each other, but with other species as well. Their
ability to communicate is legendary and the core of dolphin society. Pods of dolphins defend each other and they
hunt in a cooperative team with every individual working
toward the common good of the entire pod. Fast and sleek,
they have been known to race speed boats, make up
games, and even help drowning sailors to shore. In a dolphin pod there is not one dominate male or female, like
many other pack species; rather, they seem to make their
decisions as a group.

Octopi

The Octopus is the master of two
things. The first is their ability to perform many tasks at once with each arm
probing and searching for food or shel-
ter independently of the other seven
arms. This unique ability allows the
Octopus to perform many tasks at once while

always exploring new horizons. Science believes that a mass of nerve endings at the base of each arm actually functions as a separate mini-brain. The main brain in the back basically gives a command like "search for food," and one or more arms respond, sending the information gathered by its many suction cups back to the brain. This is a difficult concept for many people to wrap their minds around because it is such foreign concept to humans.

The second unique ability of the Octopus is being able change the color and texture of its skin at will. The master of change, it seems the Octopus is never quite happy with who he is. He can vastly change his appearance for camouflage, to express emotion, or even attract a mate. All this is going on while all eight arms are moving as well. The Octopus' brain system boggles the mind.

Crabs

Crabs are one of the hardest working creatures in the sea. Always on the move, the crab scurries here and there collecting everything they need to survive and prosper, while at the same time remaining aware of their surroundings with eyes watching for predators, competitors, and possible mates. Their protective shells and heavy armaments make them a force to be reckoned with. The industrious crabs can be found in all parts of the ocean and in fresh water sources, too. Their ability to adapt has made them great survivors.

Unlike the way Americans think of crabs, in Asia

the crab is revered as a noble creature. They adorn Asian art and there is even a martial art form based on their movements. The crab can defend itself against bigger creatures and is found all over the world, in and out of the water. They range in size from as small as a dime to as large as six feet across.

All four of these sea creatures have amazing traits that make them unique in the sea. However, they are all very different from each other not only in appearance, but in behavior and survival strategies. The shark survives by being a tireless hunter. The dolphins use relationships within the pod to prosper. The Octopus uses change and multitasking to survive. The crab is industrious, meticulous, and adaptable. If you ever had to interact with these animals, you would treat each one differently. Playing with a dolphin can be fun - playing with a shark could be dangerous. Handling an octopus could be interesting - handling a crab would be painful. This is true of the people they represent, too. The approach you use in a meeting with an octopus would not work with a crab, and vise-versa.

People in the Sea Creature Model

Now that we have a common interpretation of these sea creatures, let's look at how this metaphor relates to motivational factors in people.

Sharks

People who are identified as sharks are task driven. What makes them tick is a goal, a defined direction, a problem to overcome, or a results-driven mission. They love "to-do" lists. They don't like to waste time, money, or resources, and are driven by the idea of results. Just like a real shark, they swim until they find the opportunity, they stalk the opportunity, kill it, and eat it. Then they are onto the next opportunity. They are motivated by goals and plans. A positive result makes their day. Never ones to be idle, sharks stay active and fill their days with productive activities - they never stop swimming. The shark is powerful and can be dangerous if you get between them and their dinner (umm ... goal). People who are sharks are easily annoyed by anything that wastes their time or does not seem logical. They have a keen ability to pick out what makes sense in business from a logistics point of view. This ability is similar to real sharks in that people-sharks seem to have an extrasensory organ that helps them see the big picture. Also, once they have their eye on a target, it rarely gets away.

Dolphins

The fun loving dolphin is all about relationships. The relationship is more important to a dolphin than the goal. The dolphin is not only concerned with their own relationships, but everyone else's relationships, too. In short, they want everyone to get along and play nice. Opposed to personal conflict, the dolphin is always looking to strengthen ties and promote goodwill. They like chatting about personal issues and are usually looking out for everyone at the meeting. They have a strong sense of fair play and can easily take personal offense to any attack on them or someone else's ideas or contributions. They like to hunt as a team and gain consensus for decisions by looking at everyone's point of view. They are always looking for input and are good at gathering allies and friends to rally around any cause they back.

Their unique ability to build a strong and loyal team is a great asset to any organization. Their ability to make peace at meetings can solve many conflicts.

Octopi

Like their namesake, these people are always on the look-out for new ideas, concepts, and strategies. The arms (thoughts) are always moving in eight different directions. The octopus is rarely happy sitting still and their minds

are always active. To an octopus, no idea is perfect and no task is ever truly complete. They are always thinking of ways to change, improve, or modify the concept. The ability to be probing multiple streams of thought at the same time makes the octopus the perfect out-of-the box thinker. Most of the time, they are thinking so far out of the box that they forget where they left the box. They love new ideas and are good at spotting links between divergent ideas that others will probably miss. Also, just like a real octopus, they love change. They're not even sure what the term "status-quo" means. Changing every part of a plan is not a problem for the octopus. In fact, they love to change everything because it gives their minds the opportunity to dream up something completely new.

Crabs

People who are identified as crabs are detail oriented, industrious, and persistent. They love organization and systems. With a true understanding of processes, the crab is the glue that keeps things from falling apart. Unique among all the types, the crab actually enjoys the minutia that is needed in creating a well running company, system or process. They want things to be documented and are good at creating repeatability in the workplace. Crabs are polishers, always trying to create perfection in their work and the work of others. No detail is too small to escape their ever watchful eye. They are great at proofing or double checking facts and data for accuracy. Great with money and other numeric information, the crab is a great organizer who enjoys their job.

The crab also has the unique ability to spot problems and pit falls well before they happen. Since their minds work in a process, when a new concept is brought to the table, the crabs start to envision how the idea will be implemented. If there is a rough spot in the plan, they will bring it up early with a reality check for everyone at the meeting.

Weaknesses and Shortcomings

For a company to survive and prosper, all four types of people are needed. The octopus dreams up new ideas. The shark spots the good octopus ideas, makes a plan, and gets things moving. The crab gathers up the mess left by the shark's feeding frenzy and organizes it into a repeatable system. Meanwhile, the dolphins keep the other three from killing each other in the process. Maybe it was God's plan, but by birth the human race is the perfect team. Working together, there is nothing the four types can't achieve. Getting them to work together, however, is sometimes a difficult process. I find it interesting that as a population, humans are broken up into 40% dolphins, 30% crabs, 20-25% sharks, and 5-10% octopi. This is pretty much the perfect make up for any team or company. Now, if we can just get the humans to understand that they are the perfect team, we'll all be better off.

In the last section, I talked about the strengths of each motivational type, but I didn't discuss the weaknesses. Nobody is perfect, and none of the four types are perfect either. There are strong and weak elements to everything in nature. Let's take a quick look at each group's shortcomings so you can start to see why so many meeting go astray.

Sharks

The shark likes to get things done. Because of this, they can be short-tempered, intolerant, or even mean. Focused only on the task, they often don't take the emotional needs of the other types into account. The other types can see the sharks as standoffish or rude, or feel like the sharks don't have time for them. The shark, without meaning to, can hurt people's feelings, alienate employees or clients, and lower morale. Since they are relatively thick skinned themselves, they assume that everyone else is, too. As a manager, they are often seen as the "crack the whip" type. They can come off as pushy know-it-all's who want their own way all the time. They don't like to follow, they like to lead, and in a follower position they can often make the leader nervous or angry, even leader who are also sharks. Despite the shark's amazing talents, if they don't temper these shortcomings, it can lead to all of their hard work crumbling at their fins.

Dolphins

Where the shark doesn't worry about people's feelings, the dolphin worries too much. Their hyper-important view of relationships can often get in the way of getting the job done. They hate to fire people and will hang onto bad employees far longer than any other personality types. Their need for consensus can slow processes down to a crawl and create a slow moving, clumsy organization. Other types can view the dolphin as wishy-washy or indecisive. Their need to cement relations at work can sometimes lead to poor productivity - there are just too many birthday celebrations going on. In a meeting, their need to get everyone onboard with their ideas can make for very long, drawn out process. Their strengths in developing relationships are a double-edged sword. They build very strong bonds, but in the process these bonds can get in the way of solid, logical decisions.

Octopi

The Octopus is very hard to pin down. They always want to build in extra options with any plan. Due to the large number of ideas floating around in their heads at any given time, they can appear like a butterfly catcher in a field swarming with butterflies. It's often difficult to get them to catch just one butterfly and allow the rest of the butterflies to get away. An octopus' mind is unique among all the four types in that the scientific community believes they are actually born with a mind that functions differently than that of the other types. It's difficult for them to stay on one line of thought for very long. This can make them appear scatter-brained or even hyper-active. In meetings, they will often want to veer off the agenda into areas that the meeting was never intended to cover. Not great with details, the octopus' work can seem careless and sloppy to others.

Since the octopus is by far the minority of the types (less then 10% of the population), they often feel excluded, rejected, or out of the loop. Their tendency for paranoia can lead to the octopus withdrawing from the group or giving up and just going along with the flow with a "collect the paycheck and go home" attitude.

Crabs

The crab's need for accuracy can drive the people around them crazy. They can seem needlessly nit-picky and harsh. They are easily annoyed by minor problems and can completely dismiss ideas over a spelling mistake or a transposed 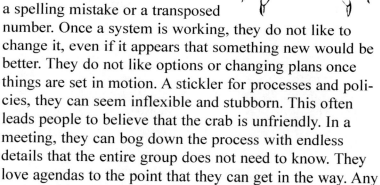 number. Once a system is working, they do not like to change it, even if it appears that something new would be better. They do not like options or changing plans once things are set in motion. A stickler for processes and policies, they can seem inflexible and stubborn. This often leads people to believe that the crab is unfriendly. In a meeting, they can bog down the process with endless details that the entire group does not need to know. They love agendas to the point that they can get in the way. Any deviance from the agenda is seen as intolerable to the crab.

Because the crab can see pitfalls well in advance, they are often seen as idea killers and can be viewed as a "stick-in-the-mud." This can make them unpopular with other creatures, especially octopi.

Looking at the types from a weaknesses point of view, it doesn't make any of them look very good, does it? Nothing could be farther from the truth. Every type brings excellence to the meeting table as long as they are understood and managed in a way that is consistent with their type and allows them to bring out their strengths. Failure to identify and/or communicate with the different types correctly can have horrendous consequences. This is why this information is so important for becoming "Meeting Royalty". Imagine a meeting where some people speak English, others Spanish, some Chinese, and the rest Russian, and there are no interpreters present. Can you envision what a mess that would be? This is exactly what is happening in many meetings. The sharks speak shark, the dolphins speak dolphin, and so on. Now, imagine that you are the interpreter. You're the one that can talk to all of them and translate for the others. Can you image how valuable you would be to that meeting?

In the next two chapters, we will be discussing how to identify and speak to the different sea creatures in their native tongues. This ability will allow you to better motivate, convince, and persuade all the groups you encounter. The power of these skills should not be underestimated.

Chapter Five
There are a Lot of Fish in the Sea

The desire for each type to communicate in their native tongue is the root of the problem in most meetings. Even in a meeting where everyone at the meeting is the same type (although rare), there is still a problem because only one view of ideas is presented. That is not a good plan for growth, stability, or success.

In the diagram 5a, you can see that I have organized the types into a wheel matrix. The spokes of the wheel

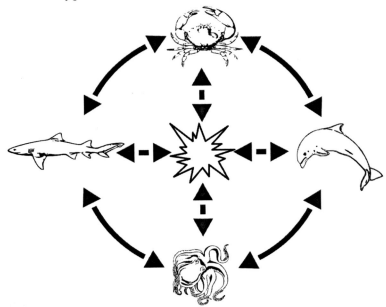

Diagram 5a

meet in an explosive middle. What this diagram is pointing out, is that types directly opposite of each other on the matrix clash the most. So, sharks and dolphins butt heads, as do crabs and octopi. As future "Meeting Royalty", this is important for you to note, monitor, and prevent. Two opposite types going at it in a meeting can derail any chance of success.

To begin the process, you first need to analyze yourself. What creature are you? There may be two that you lean toward, but think it out until you pick the one that is the closet match for you in most cases. For instance, I am an octopus, but have I shark tendencies. I LOVE new ideas, but I like to get things done, too. However, when push comes to shove in a meeting, my octopus side of myself is the one that will always shine through.

Once you have identified yourself, you may start to realize that you talk the talk for the creature you are. More importantly, you carry the biases of the creature you are. If you're a shark, dolphins probably drive you crazy, but that's probably because you've never taken the time to understand them. That's what I'm going to ask you to do: understand the enemy. It's also important to empathize, communicate, and see things from their point of view. Is this an easy thing to do? Of course not! But this is an essential step you need to take if you want to maximize your effectiveness.

Let's look at the biases of each animal.

What Sharks Think of Dolphins

- A waste of my valuable time

- Indecisive
- Wishy-washy
- Too touchy-feely
- Too dependent
- Needy
- Needs too much supervision

What Dolphins Think of Sharks

- Uncaring
- Doesn't have the time for me
- Wants everything their way
- Bossy/Pushy
- Know-it-all
- Rushed
- Unfriendly

What Crabs Think of Octopi

- They're all over the place
- Scatter-brained
- Sloppy
- Don't care about their work
- Poor quality work
- Total lack of focus
- Never gets anything done on time
- Doesn't take things seriously

What Octopi Think of Crabs

- Inflexible
- Set in their ways
- Nit-picky

- Mean
- Hates me/Doesn't understand me
- Uncreative
- Boring
- Pain in the ... well you know

With these biases, is it any wonder that a lot of meetings are so ineffective? You have the dolphins driving the sharks crazy with unrelated stories about their cat, the sharks are ticking the dolphins off with their cold demeanors, the crabs believe the octopi should be fired immediately, and the octopi are falling asleep during the crab's budget briefing. This is hardly a recipe for success.

What if we looked at the creatures in different way? What if we looked at their strengths instead of their weaknesses? What if we looked at everyone's highest intentions? Would it make a difference? Let's look at those lists again with my comments added below each shortcoming.

What Sharks Think of Dolphins

- They're wasting my valuable time
    No they're not, they're learning to trust you so they can trust your decisions and ideas. Once they trust you, working with them will be easier.
- They can't make a decision
    Yes they can, they are just analyzing as much feedback as possible before the decision is made. This can often lead to a better decisions and superior buy-in by the staff.

- Wishy-washy
    They are just trying to consider everyone's opinions and are swayed by input. As more information becomes available, they can change their minds often.
- Too touchy-feely
    Yes they are. That's something be valued since it generates closer relationships with other dolphins and octopi.
- Too dependent
    They just want to know where you stand on the issues.
- Needy
    They are just craving your input. See this as a compliment.
- Needs too much supervision
    As always, they just want your input and feedback. This is important to a dolphin.

What Dolphins Think of Sharks

- Uncaring
    Sharks care very much about the goal and results. That's good thing, it means they are working hard.
- Doesn't have the time for me
    They don't even have the time for themselves, let alone you. It's not personal, they are just busy.
- Wants everything their way
    It might take a shark awhile to come to a conclusion, but once they have they are 100% convinced they are right. Since they

want everything to turn out well, they will
fight for their ideas. They just have convic-
tion which is a good trait.

- Bossy/Pushy

    This is just a symptom of knowing what
    their goal is.

- Know-it-all

    Not true. A shark won't comment if they
    don't know what they are talking about.
    But, once they're sure, they are going to
    push their ideas with confidence. Being
    confident is different than being a know-it-
    all.

- In a rush

    Yep, they are. They still have eight things
    on their to-do list to complete before the
    day is over. If a shark doesn't complete their
    daily list, they feel like they failed. As a
    dolphin, you don't want them to feel like a
    failure, do you?

- Unfriendly

    It's not that they're unfriendly, trust me they
    know how to party, it's just that when they
    work, they work, and when they play, they
    play. There is no in-between for them. In a
    meeting they are just in their work mode.
    Invite them for dinner sometimes and you'll
    see how friendly they can be.

What Crabs Think of Octopi

- They're all over the place

    Remember, that's the way their minds work:

they have multiple streams of thought all the time. It allows them to see connections that others often miss.

- Scatter-brained

    No, it's just while you were on one thought they jumped ahead to another and are considering things at a different angle. Always keep in mind that they might just be right.

- Sloppy

    While this is true, it's because they are focused on the idea, not the execution. If they are typing up a document, their fingers can't type fast enough to keep up with the flow of ideas spewing from their brain. Cut them some slack. A misspelled word is easily fixed; a missed idea is gone forever.

- Doesn't care about their work

    -They care very much - very much! They care about the idea or concept. Whether the word should have been spelled "their" instead of "there" is just not that important to them. The new idea could save or make the company a lot of money,

- Poor quality work

    See the two comments above.

- Lack of focus

    The octopus has more focus than you can possibly imagine. The difference between the two of you, is they are focusing on at least three different ideas all at once. It's a unique quality that makes them who they are.

- Never gets anything done on time

They get a lot done, just not one thing at a time. The best way for an octopus to work is to flesh out the ideas and then let a detail specialist like a crab clean it up and make it presentable. Look at it this way: they are keeping you employed with lots of work to do.

- Doesn't take things seriously

    Because they are not tied down by rules or regulations, the idea of "breaking the rules" doesn't bother them. Following the rules is too constrictive for an octopus. Rules are good things within reason, but sometimes breaking them is the best course of action.

What Octopi Think of Crabs

- Inflexible

    They're just trying to keep things organized. They don't break the rules, but they will make new rules if necessary. It just has to be documented first.

- Stuck in their ways

    They believe in doing things by the book. The book was written for a reason and you need to understand the rules before you can understand when to break them. Crabs know the rules, so listen to them.

- Nit-picky

    There is nothing wrong with perfection. Attention to detail is what makes a quality product and crabs do it better than anyone.

- Mean

No, they just don't like the octopus' haphazard way of doing things. It pushes their buttons. Feeding the crabs one bite at a time instead of an entire smorgasbord at once works much better.

- Hates me/Doesn't understand me

    This can be true, but it's really more the case that they don't like it when you gloss over the details. They are looking at the tree while you're looking at the forest, and the ocean, and the planet Saturn, and the next door neighbor's dog ...

- Uncreative

    This is definitely not true. They are very creative when it comes to putting together processes and step-by-step plans. It's their gift.

- Boring

    They're into the details. They just want to inventory every tree by type and age. When you need this information for your wild octopus ideas, you'll be glad they collected it.

- Pain in the ... well you know

    They just think differently than you do, that's all. By taking the time to understand them and allowing them to put your ideas into play, you will start to get along.

Isn't that a better way of viewing things? The next time you're at a meeting and someone is beginning to rub you the wrong way, ask yourself what creature they are and remember this chapter. Look at the situation or problem from their point of view and empathize, understand, and change your meeting style to match. You'll be surprised how much better off you'll be. In fact, the opposite types actually need each other the most. Have you ever heard the term, "opposites attract?"

I know from my point of view that crabs can drive me up the wall. I'm an octopus, after all. The stream of mind-numbing details combined with worrying about problems way down the road really cramps my style. However, I know I need to work closely with crabs in order to have a successful outcome for the company in the long run. That's why I have to keep my octopusness (that's not a word, is it?) in check when speaking with them. I need to realize that they need to have the details and step-by-step plans in order to feel comfortable with the decision. My need to bring them on-board with my decisions is more important than my need to always be an octopus.

Here is the big "ah hah!" moment for this chapter. You can't be "Meeting Royalty" unless you are sometimes willing to bend and put aside your favorite way of working. You would not believe the amount of resistance I get to this concept, especially from kings and queens. The attitude of "I'm in charge and I'll do it my way," can really get in the way. It's far easier to change yourself than it is to change everyone else. After all, there is only one of you and five billion, nine hundred and ninety-nine million, nine hundred and ninety-nine thousand, nine hundred and ninety-nine others people in the world. Doesn't it make more sense just to change yourself?

Leaders need to be able to facilitate success in

meetings. Be the one that can swallow your pride and play the game to win. If you find yourself saying "I can't," or, "I won't do that," as you read on, add "because I don't want to be an effective leader," at the end of your sentence. After you hear yourself say that a couple of times, it will start to annoy you and you'll drop your objections and get with the program. In Dale Carnegie's famous book, "How to Make Friends and Influence People", he talks about a man who drives toward an intersection knowing he has the right-of-way. He sees a car coming, but he has the right-of-way so he keeps right on going. Although he was right, he is still dead. Sharks, crabs, and to some extent, octopi, have this "right at any cost" attitude and even though it can serve them well sometimes, it can keep them from becoming the extraordinary leader they could be. A shark king or queen is at the most risk for falling into the "I can't bend" trap. Check your ego at the door because we have a lot more ground to cover.

Chapter Six
Identifying What's in the Net

How do you identify the different personality types in a meeting? The ability to identify individual creatures quickly is more than half the battle. The different creatures can't help but expose themselves for who they are once you know the tell-tale signs of each creature. I've gotten to the point where I can be 90% convinced of my guess within the first two minutes of talking to someone. This is useful for even short meetings. There are a number of ways to spot someone's type. You can observe language, body stance, and facial expressions, all of which we will discuss in this chapter. But first, let's review the creatures and boil them down into their essences.

Sharks - Goal oriented, results driven, time sensitive.
Dolphins - Relationship oriented, friendship driven, likes to work in teams.
Octopi - Crazy about new ideas and concepts, loves to dream up new stuff.
Crabs - Detail oriented, plan based.

First, let discuss language. There are certain phrases or themes in speech that the different types like to use. When you spot it, take note of the person and their possible sea creature type. Just one statement shouldn't make you jump to conclusions, but you should then be on the look out for other phrases to solidify your guess. Below are some common speech patterns to look for in each type.

Sharks

"Can we move this along?"

"So what's your point?"

"How will this affect the bottom line?"

"Can I see your proof of that?"

"Show me your track record."

"So let's cut to the chase."

"We have to hurry; I don't have a lot of time."

"We need to stay on schedule."

"So how much money (time, etc) can we save?"

Note that all of these phrases have something to do with results or time. In the rush, rush, rush world of sharks they need to keep things moving and maximize effectiveness. Look for statements that suggestion this motivation.

Example e-mail from a shark:

I can meet Thursday from 3:10 to 3:35 or Friday from10:15 to 10:45. Let my assistant know by the end of today's business.

-Jim Diceman, CFO

      In the email above, note how straight to the point the message was. No pleasantries, just information about what needs to get done. Notice the precise mention of and expectation of time. Time is very important to sharks. It's imperative that you don't waste their time as well. On the signature line, note the full name and title. The title is important because it is the result of all their hard work.

      When responding to such an email, keep it brief and to the point. They will appreciate that.

Dolphins

"Let's get to know each other."

"We should do this over lunch."

"It's so nice to meet you in person."

"We need to form a committee."

"We should get a group consensus."

"I can't wait to see you again."

"Do you have some time next week to chat?"

"Can you talk to Bob, Carol, and Janis about this idea?"

"It sounds like a good idea, what do you think?"

Notice that all the dolphin statements have to do with spending more time with you and bringing in more people. To a dolphin, the bigger the circle of players, the better.

Example e-mail from a dolphin:
Hi!

It was so nice to meet you the other day. I was hoping we could get together and get to know each other better. I was so sorry to hear that your dog needs surgery, please let me know how it goes. I hope that Fluffy is going to be ok.

We need to get together next week sometime, whenever it is convenient for you, to talk about the Jackson account. Let me know what works best for you and I'll rearrange my schedule. Maybe I can get Jerry and Margaret in on a conference call. I would love to hear their thoughts on the marketing theme for next year.

Well, I have to go. Please let me know when you can chat next week and say hi to your lovely wife for me.

Thanks so much!

-Susan

Note the use of exclamation points. They accent the personal connection phrases. The first paragraph has nothing to do with the issue at hand; its only function is to let you know they care. When setting up the meeting, they don't want to put any pressure on you to comment. The phrase "I'll rearrange my schedule," is common in dolphin language. They want you to feel accommodated. The signature of only the first name, or even a nickname, is typical.

Your reply should be written in the same style. A few extra paragraphs will be well worth the effort in order to make the dolphin feel comfortable.

Octopi

"I've got a GREAT idea!" (Note the exclamation point)

"I just thought this up ..."

"Can you repeat that? I missed it."

"What if we took a completely different approach?"

"Now there's an interesting idea!"

"Let's brainstorm."

"Let toss it all out and start over."

"What if we did a complete 180..."

"If you could have anything you wanted, what would it be?"

"I'm bored with this topic, what else can we talk about?"

"I saw this web-site that lets you create your own sound system from 180,000 options!"

The octopi comments are always focused on new thought, imaginary concepts, or change. They can often use a lot of excitement in their phrases. New ideas are like crack to an octopus. Also, look for them to be involved in a lot of unrelated activities. Octopi become bored easily and like a lot of diverse functions or hobbies in their lives.

Example e-mail from an octopus:

Hey,

I woke up a few minutes ago with this incredible idea for the Jackson account and I just had to share it right away. What if we painted the entire building bright red with a couple of eyeballs on the side? It could be called the "Red Eye on 9th Street" building! Cool, huh?

Oh yeah! I'll mock it up in photo-paint and have it

ready for you to look at in the morning. Let's pitch it to the client tomorrow.

See you bright and early,

Amele

Yes, our friend the octopus is at it again. It's hard to get through an email without a new idea or options to consider. Once they get an idea in their heads they want to share it as soon as possible. This is probably the greatest idea that there has ever been, at least to the octopus. An octopus' email can seem jolting, especially when they want to jump the gun, like in the second paragraph. As with the dolphin email, there are exclamation points, but this time they are accenting ideas, not the personal connections. It is very common to only have a first name signature or no signature at all.

When responding to a message like this, be sure not to crush their ideas. Octopi become very attached to their ideas and dismissing them straight out can be offensive. However, if you don't think it's a terribly good idea, be sure to temper your enthusiasm; otherwise, you might wake up to one red building with eyes and an extremely irate client.

Crabs

"Do you have this in writing?"

"Let's see your data."

"Send me all your information and we'll schedule a new meeting."

"What are all the steps?"

"Please clarify."

"Next time use your grammar checker. Yikes."

"That won't work."

"That's not in the budget."

"Write this up for me and put it in my mail box."

"I want to go over the contract line by line."

"Run the numbers for me with all 29 parameters."

Notice the theme for the crab. It's all detail and documentation based. Also, their first reaction to almost any concept would be to point out what is wrong with it.

Example e-mail from a Crab:

Dear Janice,

Have you read the email from Amele yet? I have esti-mated that painting the Jackson building bright red would cost $22,000 and there is no money in the budget for that. Plus, there is a city zoning clause that states that all buildings on 9th street have to be a *neutral color. The zoning ordinance is CO123-34B. Lastly, there are a number of large windows on the side of the building and unless you want to paint over the windows, the big eyes on the building won't work. Please call me before you talk to Amele at 456-356-1231 ext. 121 or on my cell at 456-879-3323, or after 5:30 p.m. at 456-232-1123.*

Jerry M. Sidwell
O: 456-356-1231 ext 121
C: 456-879-3323
F: 456-356-1247

As always, the crab is looking ahead for pitfalls in the idea and has already spotted some big ones. Not one to mince words, they are getting right to their objections with detailed reasoning and evidence as to why they are right. Precise ways to contact her are presented in the email twice, once in the body of the text and again in the signature. This is almost always the type of signature that you will find on a crab's e-mail, although other creature types may have the same type of thing in their signatures because of the nature of email software. So, this type of signature in and of itself is not enough to spot a crab.

Always, always, always acknowledge their points in your reply. Maybe painting the building red is a fantastic idea, and there might be ways around the problems, but the problems are valid and the crab needs to be acknowledged for spotting them. Never tackle the issues in e-mail; discussions with a crab work much better over the phone or face-to-face. Always thank them for bringing the issues to your attention; after all, you wouldn't want to spend a lot of money painting the building red only to be fined by the city and have to repaint it the original color again.

Body Language and Facial Expression Identifiers

Don't put too much credence in this method, because it doesn't always work, but it is a good way to confirm what you are already thinking. If you think a person may be a dolphin, and they have some tell-tale body language signs of a dolphin, it can help you to reach a conclusion more quickly. The problem with any system that relies only on body language factors is that many times people give misleading signs because of the way they feel that day, health concerns, or a host of other factors that have nothing to do with what you are trying to rate. I personally cross my arms sometimes, not because I'm closed off to ideas, but just because I don't know what else to do with my arms. A good rule of thumb would be to only give these techniques about a 20% weight on your decision. They are helpful, but only in order to cement your choice.

That being said, I stay aware of this concept most of the time. Earlier in the book, I stated that I can read most people in any meeting within the first ten minutes. What I'm about to share with you helps me do that. So, let's take a quick look at what body and facial expressions can give you glues to someone's creature type.

Sharks

When seated, sharks normally sit up straight with their backs against the chair. Their hands are often folded on the desk. If they have documentation, it is organized in front of them for easy retrieval. Eye contact is solid and consistent. Facial expressions are minimal and they only laugh if the joke is really good.

When standing, look for the shark's stance to be straight on to you. Posture is usually good with their hands at their sides or behind their back. Sharks rarely talk with their hands.

Dolphins

When seated, the dolphin spends most of their time sitting in a relaxed position. One or both elbows are on the table, or their hands are in their lap. Dolphins like to smile and laugh, so look for a lot of facial expressions. They wear their feelings on the face and will show displeasure and frustration just as much as they will show happiness. They are prone to speaking with their hands.

When standing, look for them to take a sideways stance to yours. It's a less confrontational stance and dolphins hate confrontation.

Octopi

The octopus will sit in any style, but their favorite is leaning back in the chair or leaning forward with their back off the chair. This is a gage of how interested they are in the topic. When they get excited, they lean forward. Notes are often scattered in front of them and they can have trouble finding what they are looking for.

The octopus likes to fidget with things like pencils, or paper clips. Even if they are not holding anything, their fingers are often moving most of the time.

Octopi can appear stone-faced when they are bored, or they can light up like a Christmas tree when they are excited. They will often talk with both eyebrows raised or constantly moving.

Crabs

Like the shark, the crab sits up with their back against the chair, notes organized, and they utilize little facial expressions. This can make it difficult to distinguish between the crabs and sharks. Look for indicators other than physicality to choose between the two.

Chapter Seven
Talking Sea Creature

L et's bring it all together now by discussing how to converse in the different sea creature tongues. Once you have identified what type a person is, you will then be able to talk to them with language that will be of interest to them and that they will readily understand. This is similar to being able to speak French to a person from France. Even if the Frenchmen speaks English, he will understand you a lot better if you are speaking French.

This chapter will show you how to add phrases to your language that will help you better connect with the different types and give you the ability to translate from one creature language to another. This ability will make you invaluable to any meeting.

Sharks

Here are phrases to include when talking to sharks:

"The bottom line is ..."

"As a result ..."

"This worked before at ..."

"The benefits are ..."

"To cut to the chase ..." or *"To get to the point ..."*

"To summarize what's been said ..."

"We need to move this along ..."

"In a nut shell ..."

Starting a sentence with any of these phrases will get a shark's attention. It's like a drop of blood in the water - they can't help but notice. Keep this in mind as we discuss how to translate the other languages into Shark.

Translating Dolphin into Shark

Sharks become frustrated with dolphins easily. They just don't see the need for all the touchy-feely experiences. When translating Dolphin into Shark, you need to point out how a better relationship will add to more sales, better profits, increased efficiency, or decreased waste. Sharks can often overlook the human factor, which is what dolphins are good at. When you sense the shark is becoming annoyed by the constant storytelling and long explanations of the dolphin, summarize what the dolphin said in a quick results-driven statement. Statements such as:

"I think what Susan is trying to say is that the bottom line is that if our departments communicate better we will drastically cut down on mistakes. We can do this by getting them to think more like one team."

"To summarize what Bob has eloquently pointed out, we need to reach out to the community so they can understand our mission. That could lead to more sales."

Boil down the main points and put a result-orientated spin on it. This will get the shark engaged with the dolphin and make them want to hear more.

Translating Octopus into Shark

In general, sharks understand and appreciate octopi. They realize that out-of-the-box thinking leads to profitable ideas. However, they can sometimes become frustrated with octopi when they can't focus on just one idea. Here is what happens: the octopus presents a myriad of ideas and the shark spots a good one. He wants to flesh out the idea, but the octopus is too excited to stop his explosion of ideas and focus on just one of them. This is normally a two part translation. First, you have to stop the onslaught of ideas from the octopus and then get the two of them focused on the best, or most manageable idea.

"Let me break in a second here Martha. To cut to the chase, what are your three favorite options?"

Listen for the answer and then turn to the shark and ask:

"Out of those three, what is your favorite one, John?"

Even if one of the three ideas is not John's favorite,

this gives the shark the opportunity to take the floor and get things moving again.

Translating Crab into Shark

Sharks value crabs because they understand how much they need them. The only problem is that crabs like to beat a dead horse into a bloody stump. The crab leaves no stone unturned and wants to share all the great research work they have done. When looking at a forest, the crabs see every tree and bush. When looking at the forest, the shark sees a tree that they can process into a 2x4 piece of lumber. The shark doesn't need all the details, he trusts the crab; he just wants the conclusion the crab came to. The crab is getting there, just not in the time frame the shark would like.

We can actually have the crabs translate for themselves if we give them the chance. It's important to give the sharks the information they are looking for, but still show appreciation for the crabs. Say this to the crab:

> *"Wow, this is an amazing amount of data you've collected. Unfortunately, we don't have time during our meeting to hear it all. Could you get us a copy of your data? That would be great. In a nutshell, what conclusion did your research lead you to?"*

Stand back and let the crab summarize.

Dolphins

Intros to dolphin sentences sound like this:

"What we need to get together and do ..."

"As a team we can ..."

"Let's work together ..."

"Can we get everyone to agree ..."

"How do you feel about ..."

"Let's take some time and consider ..."

"How will this affect the employees ..." (or clients, community, individuals, etc.)

"What is your gut reaction ..."

Dolphins like to feel connected. Notice that all of these phrases have that in common. The last phrase, "what is your gut reaction," sometimes throws people, but dolphins swim instinctively and they know how they feel about any situation pretty quickly. Letting them express their feelings is important in understanding dolphins and having influence with them.

Translating Shark into Dolphin

Dolphins get along well with most people with the

exception of sharks. In a meeting, dolphins and sharks can get into a knock-down drag out brawl if left to their own devices. Or, the shark can run over the dolphin, leaving them feeling resentful or angry. Dolphins have a unique trait that is something to be wary of if you are a shark: if a dolphin gets into a fight at a meeting, they carry those feelings outside the meeting and it can affect relationships for months, if not years. Sharks, on the other hand, think that business is business. They can fight it out in a meeting, and then invite the person to lunch as soon as the meeting is over. This dichotomy in personal styles leads to real problems with sharks and dolphins. Sharks should take careful note of this because dolphins are the majority of the population. The quick, fast paced, "get it done now," approach of a shark lands cold with dolphins.

When translating shark to dolphin, keep a close eye on the dolphins and watch for any adverse reactions to shark statements. A shark has no problem saying something like:

"If we cut twenty percent of the staff, then we can ..."

The sharks have just sent the dolphins into uncharted levels of frustration. You will be able to see the look of shock on the dolphins' faces. As a good translator, you need to break in and stop this train wreck in its tracks. It will annoy the sharks to some extent, but you need to stop their flow and allow the dolphins to catch up. Say something along the lines of:

"Hold on a second Rich, how did you come to the

conclusion that we need to cut twenty percent of the staff?"

It could be that cutting staff is the only way to achieve the company's goals, but such a move will be painful for dolphins. They need to hear the arguments for such a move in order to have any chance of buying in. After hearing Rich's logic, turn to the lead dolphin and suggest:

"Peggy, do you think you and Rich could form a team and see if there are any other alternatives?"

Dolphins like teams. An idea verified by a team will carry far more weight with dolphins than a shark's directive. Now, get your shark back in the game.

"Ok, we'll table that idea for now. Rich, let's hear the rest of your plan."

Once Rich is back on his way, he will forget about the interruption and revert to business as usual. Meanwhile, the dolphin will have felt heard and have time to get used to the idea. The argument has been avoided.

Translating Octopus into Dolphin

As with the shark, the fast pace of an octopus can sometimes run over a dolphin. The octopus moves faster than any other type. They don't go from A to B; they go from A to H to a circle to the color red and then back to B. This can be hard for the other creatures to follow. The energy of their ideas can take away from the people-oriented focus of the dolphin. The important thing to keep in mind is to always put the people-oriented element back into the ideas. If the octopus makes a statement like:

> *"I just saw this great new graphics design system that blows what we're using away. In the next two months, we should convert all our systems over to it."*

I can guarantee you that the first thing that ran through the dolphin's mind was the people issue. What about training? What about people's fear of change? How will this affect the design staff? Once again, we need to slow down the enthusiasm of the octopus from light-speed to a speed that's more manageable. Say something like this to the octopus:

> *"I'd love to see a demo of the software as soon as possible, but have you considered what effect this change will have on the staff."*

This is what the dolphin needs to discuss and you just gave them a perfect opportunity to do so. There is a good chance that the octopus has not considered this question. The octopus will not like being ground to a halt (in the octopus' view), but losing all the dolphins in the room to make the octopus happy is not a good idea. Plus, once the octopus hears everyone else's input their minds will be flying to solve all the obstacles to the plan, which will keep them occupied and happy.

Translating Crab into Dolphin

Although dolphins can, at times, get bore by the

amount of detail brought to the table by crabs, they generally get along with this type and communication between the groups works pretty well. Very little translation is needed for the two types.

Octopus

The octopus is about speed, ideas, and change. This is what lights them up. The problem is that the octopus often needs to be reined in, which they don't like. Their "idea factory" mentality is hard to stop once it gets started. The best way to communicate with an octopus is to give them new concepts to consider, or new ideas to conjure up. As long as an octopus is thinking, they're happy. Knowing this, translating to octopus can be rather easy. Basically any phrase that gets them thinking will keep the octopus engaged. Try these phrases:

"We need ideas for ..."

"What options could we apply ..."

"How could we modify this ..."

"If you could have anything you wanted ..."

"If budget were not a constraint ..."

"How could we ..."

"Can you dream up ..."

Note that almost all of these phrases are in the form

of a question or a request. This is the best way to not only engage the octopus, but also the to utilize their unique talents.

Translating Shark into Octopus

The octopus always wants an option. When a shark is in authority (say a rook or queen) and gives an order, the poor octopus feels stifled. They will do the task, but they won't feel like they are part of the process. The step A, step B, step C plan leaves them very little room to utilize their abilities. If you can add in even small variables to the order, it can really give the octopus something to sink its teeth into.

So if the shark says, *"We are going to paint it purple,"* it will be purple and the octopus won't mind. The point is, the octopus won't be excited either. This would work better:

> *"I want it painted purple. Can you dream up some shades or finishes and be prepared to show them to me tomorrow?"*

You have just made the octopus' day.

Translating Dolphin into Octopus

We need to remember that, due to the unique way the octopus' brain works, they often feel like outsiders. They don't need teams to do their jobs; they are quite comfortable working alone and often prefer it that way. Teams can often dampen their enthusiasm. The octopus needs to know that their ideas are not going to be squished by a committee. There is an old saying: "a camel is just a race horse designed by a committee." If you can make the octopus feel that their ideas will be heard and considered, you will have them on board.

Therefore, instead of saying, "We are going to add you to the planning committee," give them something to do for the group. Such as:

"We are going to add you to the planning committee. Can you come up with a list of ideas for the Jackson job and circulate them to the members before the next meeting?"

Now you're talking. You have just supercharged the octopus. They will work overtime for free. You'd better take at least a little time and review that list at the beginning of the planning committee meeting, though.

Translating Crab into Octopus

The day you learn to do this, you are truly "Meeting Royalty". Crabs like systems. Octopi hate systems. Crabs don't like change. Octopi love change! Crabs enjoy a limited set of options. You guessed it: octopi want as many options as possible. As much as sharks and dolphins clash, the battle between crabs and octopi is worse.

It is common to see octopi and crabs glaring at each other from across the table. If you really want to see fireworks, get an octopus queen in a room with a crab queen and watch them go at it. The Ali-Frazier fights were nothing compared to this.

When a crab starts to give an overly detailed explanation, the octopus will often zone out. Unfortunately, some of what the crab is saying are things that the octopus needs to hear. Watch for the glassy eyed, far-off look of the octopus and try and find any way to bring the octopus back in to the conversation with a question, or by asking them for an opinion.

The other problem arises when the crab brings up objections or problems with the octopus' ideas. This is a little easier to translate by saying to the crab, *"that's a good point, write that down and we can discuss it later."* Then let the octopus continue.

Crabs

Crabs want details. They like to know the background information for everything. They like to have a set plan to which everyone will adhere. Anything that deviates from organization and preciseness can set the crab off. They want everyone else to be the same way. If you don't want to lead the project, a shark will be more than happy to do it for you; if you don't want to be organized, a crab will do it for you, but will probably resent you for it. It takes more than just speaking their language to translate for crabs. Therefore, I have found that the best way to reach the crab is to make sure they feel valued. Use phrases like:

"Your plan is great! This is going to allow us to ..."

"The benefits for your organization will ..."

"Your insight was spot on ..."

"You would be the best person to ..."

I teach team building seminars based on sea creature technology. During one such seminar, I broke the group up into the four types. One of the exercises I had them do is to tell the other groups what they are sorry for. For instance, the dolphins told people they were sorry for taking so much time yakking around the water cooler. The sharks apologized for being so pushy, etc. When it came time for the crabs, they said: "we are sorry for being right all the time." Everyone laughed, but there is an element of truth to the statement. Crabs do think they are right, most of the time, if not all of the time. When they are right, it's good to acknowledge that you noticed.

Translating Shark into Crab

The sharks want to get to the point. Details are not the shark's strong suit. This can cause the shark to run over the crab on his way to the goal. Unfortunately, crabs can be hard to read. Unlike dolphins, they can be upset and not show it. Therefore, you need to anticipate the crab's desires with little, if any, clues. If the shark is doing the shark thing:

> *"We need to cut all budgets by 15% by Thursday. All team leaders need to have staffing allocations in place to cover the shortfall with ..."*

The shark is swimming fast to the goal, but the crab may not see the step by step process. Generalized statements like *"leaders need to have staffing allocations in place,"* is too general for the crab. What does that mean? The shark may not have even thought it all out yet, but the crab needs to. Slow the shark down and make him or her clarify the statement.

> *"Exactly what do you mean by staffing allocation?"*

You don't need to say anything to the crab; the shark's clarification will be enough.

Translating Dolphin into Crab

The easy going dolphins don't usually have any issues when talking to crabs. They understand them. The crab's need for plans, structure, and detail will be embraced by dolphins and therefore the crab will be happy. It's the accommodating nature of dolphin that causes this understanding.

Translating Octopus into Crab

Here we go again. These two just do not get along. The octopus is squirming all over the place, wanting to change every plan and function; meanwhile, the crabs are losing their minds. It is common for crabs to think that the octopus is the worst employee or member of the team. This translation is difficult at best. Slowing down the octopus just frustrates the octopus, but the speed and multiple directions of the octopus is madding to the crab. Don't slow down the octopus. It interferes with their thought process and some great ideas could be lost.

Here is the Catch-22 of the situation: you need to slow the octopus down, but it's not a good idea. If possible, it is a good idea to meet with the crabs ahead of time and get them to understand how the octopus works. Tell them to write down all their objections or procedural problems and, if need be, the group can talk about them at the end of the meeting. Often, an octopus' ideas are a bit out there anyway and will never reach the top of the pile for being considered at all. That means that the road blocks that the crab is spotting won't even need to be discussed. This will make the meeting shorter and more productive while still allowing the octopus to freefall their way into more productive ideas.

If it sounds like you're becoming a traffic cop, well, maybe you are. A well functioning meeting is the cornerstone to a successful business. By helping everyone play nice, while at the same time understanding each other, you are aiding the productive process in ways you cannot imagine. The ability to translate can also allow you to avoid the meeting breaking down into "cliques" that will end up warring with each other. A "clique" is two or more people teaming up with the sole intent of being an obstacle to someone else or another clique in the meeting.

In the United States of America, we have a two party political system made up of Democrats and Republicans. The unfortunate truth is that these two parties have become their own cliques and have a difficult time working together. If the Democrats came out in favor of air, the Republicans would be against it. If the Republicans came out in favor of water, the Democrats would want to vote it down. Although this brings a sense of balance to the USA, it can lead to slow going social progress. A lot of this has to do with the political nature of trying to be elected, but the same thing can develop in your meetings. It's something to be aware of and watch for.

Cliques can develop outside of meetings, with people coming to the table prepared to do battle, or they can form during the meeting and a battle can erupt right there. This "us versus them" mentality is not very productive. There are a lot of reasons why cliques can develop and some of it you may not be able to do much about. Management and unions are a perfect example of this problem.

In many companies, the two groups come to the table ready to do battle. The interesting thing is that most of the problems between management and unions have to do with history not present day reality. When unions first developed, they came to be because companies were taking advantage of employees. Most of the time, this is not the case anymore, but the mindset from the early days still lingers. You cannot expect to wipe out seventy years of history in a meeting, so some cliques will be hard to dismantle. However, many cliques are not so strongly cemented.

Cliques based on motivational factors are common. These are a lot easier to avoid when you become a good translator. Cliques form across the sea creature matrix.

Dolphins and sharks, octopi and crabs, are all on opposite sides. Here is an example:

A shark unintentionally offends a dolphin. Dolphins are good at making and keeping friends and allies. The angry dolphin starts forming a group that is opposed to the shark. Before you know it, that shark can't get anything done. Every idea is a battle and it's quickly becoming a war. Sharks are not stupid, and it won't take them long to spot the central player in the quagmire. Now the shark is on the war path, something they are good at. Remember, sharks are strategic thinkers. Through a series of well placed arguments and alliances, the shark suddenly has a clique of his own. Anger builds, tempers flare, and suddenly nothing is getting done. The octopi versus crabs wars can be even be nastier if the octopus is in a position of authority.

None of this is necessary. Almost all cliques are started by misunderstandings between sea creatures. Cliques that form during a meeting can be easily eradicated by a fast thinking translator. Cliques in frequent meetings with the same participants are trickier beasts.

What I've noticed is that cliques will sit together. They often enter the room together and all sit on one side or edge of the table. Here is an easy trick to use if you are in control of the meeting. Two words: assigned seating. You can break the psychological bonds just by moving the cliques away from each other. This is a great first step in the process of getting the two (or more) sides to work together. Plus, it's fun to watch their disgruntled faces when they see who they are sitting next to.

Another possible method is to strategically have a few people arrive at the meeting room early and sit in a way that forces the cliques to break apart.

If you're new to a meeting group and you want to spot the cliques, take a chair in a place that divides the meeting table into two halves and watch where people decide to sit. The seating arrangement may mean nothing at all, but then again it may be a sign of things to come. If the two sides are looking mainly at the other side of the table and not their own side, there is a good chance you have some cliques here. A heavily confrontational atmosphere often leads to a stare down.

Dissolving cliques may be the best way to get your meetings back on track. If you are in frequent meetings with the same people, the best way to do this would be to spot the queen and/or rooks on each side and work on the problem outside of the meetings with them separately. Getting them to recognize their mutual interest, common goals, and need for each other's strengths is a great way to bring them together. A moderated meeting with just the key players may be in order. At that meeting, get the players to lay their cards on the table and really let the other side know about their gripes and their needs.

If you have not run this type of meeting before, don't use these techniques for the first time in a critical situation. Playing the moderator between the heads of two cliques can be dicey, and you could be the one that gets diced up.

If you find yourself in a one-sided meeting with

cliques, remember to translate frequently. Uncover the queens and rooks quickly, analyze their motivational factors, and start translating everything they say that seems even remotely misunderstood by the other side.

I want to leave you with this piece of information: cliques are different than an alliance. Alliances are formed based on the player's assessment of the situation or idea. The alliance forms around backing a plan and can easily shift depending on the goals of the meeting and what each player wants out of it.

A clique on the other hand is a pact that is stronger than any one idea or plan. This group sticks together, even if they don't like the idea or plan of one of the other clique members. They vote as a block and back each other up even if they feel the other person is wrong. This is the nature of cliques and why they can be very destructive to a meeting.

Chapter Eight
Keeping Track of it All

If at this point you are saying to yourself, "Whew, that is an awful lot to keep track of in a meeting," don't worry, you are not alone. It is a lot to keep track of. In time, with consistent practice, you may get to the point where you can do it all in your head. Great chess masters can track ten or more games in their heads with no problem. However, true chess masters are relatively rare compared to chess players. So too is the case with "Meeting Royalty." A meeting master is rare among the number of people who must attend meetings. Until you get to the point of mastering these abilities, there are some ways to stay organized and aid you during a meeting.

Creating a meeting diagram is a great way to help you organize your thoughts and get you thinking in a strategic way. By having the information on becoming "Meeting Royalty" at your fingertips, you can be much nimbler on your feet. If you remember back to Chapter 3, you may recall that I discussed the process of "out-think." By always being one step ahead of everyone else in the room, you orchestrate the meeting in the direction you want it to go.

A meeting diagram can be put together and referenced quickly and easily. It looks like a pretty simple drawing, almost like a doodle, so people won't even know what you are up to. That is, of course, unless they have read my book, too. Caution: never leave your meeting diagram on the table where it can be picked up and studied by others. Your assessments of other players should be for your eyes only. As "Meeting Royalty," you will understand these notes, but others may misinterpret them and your intentions. Worse yet, you may have to explain what the diagram means to someone who is not versed in the philosophy of the meeting royals. At first glance, your meeting diagram could be seen as manipulative, although it is not.

To create your meeting diagram, make a drawing of the table (see drawing 8a). Next, label the chair backs with all the names of the people in attendance. This has an additional benefit as well since it forces you to meet everyone in the room and ask them their names. This is a great way to help yourself remember them. Writing names down on a sheet of paper is also a great cheat sheet if there are a lot of people's names to remember.

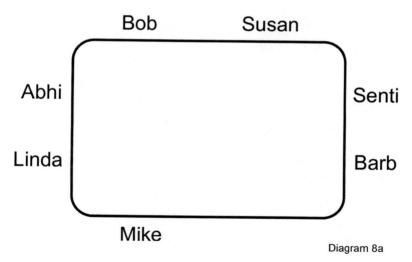

Diagram 8a

Create the meeting diagram at the start of a meeting. If you are concerned about the secrecy of the chart, you can leave the names off the chart or replace them with the first letter of the name. Another way is to put a drawing as a representative of a person. The important part is to put something on the chart that will help you quickly identify the individuals in the room.

Now, start your analysis. As you identify everyone in the room based on the chess and sea creature models, put the label in front of their names. The abbreviations for the players in the chess model are:

K - King
Q - Queen
R - Rook
B - Bishop
Kn - Knight
P - Pawn

I want to reiterate the importance of not letting the public view your diagram. Nobody likes to be thought of as a pawn, and if Carol sees your document with a P in front of her name (and Carol realizes that P stands for Pawn), you could make her mad. She shouldn't be, because almost everyone will be a pawn in some meetings they attend, but that won't help you if she is upset.

Don't worry about identifying everyone right away. Just jot down the information as you discover it. At the same time you can be identifying what their sea creature type is too. As a review, the players in the sea creature motivational factors analogy are:

S - Shark
D - Dolphin
O - Octopus
C - Crab

Here you can start to see the genius of the system, because none of the motivational factor letters duplicate the chess power structure letters. Therefore, you never have to worry about mixing them up. I usually put the power structure letter on the left and the motivational factor letter on the right, but since QS and SQ mean the same thing, it really doesn't matter which way you do it. However, I would recommend that you be consistent in your approach. It just makes it easier to recall the information. In drawing 1b, you can see a chart with all the designation in place.

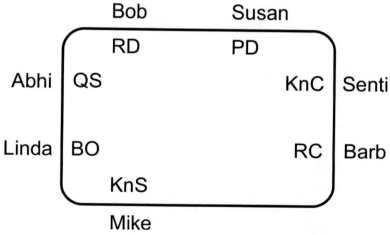

Diagram 8b

Next, you need to track the alliances. As you notice alliances forming, draw a line across your table diagram from one person to another. You can use different types of lines to represent the strength of the alliance. I use a dotted line to represent a weak bond, a solid line for a stronger one, and a double line for an alliance that may be unbreakable. Make your alliance lines across the table since you will be reserving the outside area for a different purpose.

I use the outside of the table for noting cliques. I place brackets that join the members of the clique together. It usually works out because the clique members are normally sitting next to each other. A completed chart will be similar to drawing 8c.

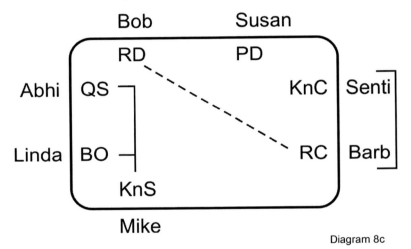

Diagram 8c

The real beauty of these diagrams is the speed at which it will help you train your mind to see meetings from this new perspective. Whenever you take a thought process and force yourself to diagram it, the act of doing so entrenches the synaptic connections in your brain three different ways. The first way is to read about it, which you are doing right now. The second mental training method is tactile, which happen when you write it down. The third reinforcement occurs during the review of your diagram. Before long you will no longer need the diagram to keep track of your meetings.

Chapter Nine
Are You Psychic?

Humans are interesting creatures. We tell people what we are thinking, even if we're not talking. We do this through facial expressions and body gestures or movements. This chapter will explain how to notice and use this information to help you manage a meeting. By knowing what people are thinking, you can alter your meeting strategy to better fit in with the desires of the players. It will seem like you're psychic.

This chapter is not a complete study of this topic. If you are interested, there are some fascinating in-depth books on this subject. Systems like NLP (Neuro-Linguistic Programming) and other methods take this topic to a completely different level. There are many other systems that study the same effect that are just as good. However, they are too complex to use during a meeting unless you have studied them most of your life. I use a useful subset of these to better understand the motivation and desires of people in meetings. There are five useful gestures that tell me almost everything I need to know about someone's mental processes. These five gestures are involuntary, and therefore hard to hide or fake, and they are universal to almost all cultures from around the world. Five gestures aren't too hard to track, are they? Anyone can notice and track five gestures.

The Head Nod

The first gesture I pay attention to is the head nod. Humans nod their heads instinctively if they agree with what they are hearing or they find it interesting. The nod can be large or very small, but it is easy to spot. This "yes" gesture is amazingly powerful if you know how to take advantage of it. Let's say you are presenting your idea for a new parking structure. During the presentation, you start getting nods from Derrick. You have already identified him as a BC (Bishop/Crab). As you already know, Bishops are influential so his approval of the plan would be a big boost to your cause. The head nod tells you that he is already interested, so what do crabs like? That's right, detail and structure. It's time to start talking about the step-by-step implementation plan for the building. Derrick is now totally on-board and we can start working on the queen.

Imagine being able to get all of this from a simple head nod. Who would have thought that was possible? This technique, combined with power structures and motivational factors, is almost like wielding a nuclear weapon. Let's look at some more examples to see the power of this technique.

You are a sales person and your company has a myriad of products, everything from soup to nuts. You begin to present your reader's digest version of what your company can provide. On your third item of a list of twenty, you get a big head nod from Danielle, a QS (Queen/Shark). We know that queens are hard to influence and their backing is critical, so you can stop the list of products right there and start talking about the one the queen liked. You can talk about the rest of the products later, but never miss a chance to get a queen on-board. She's a shark, and what do sharks like? Start talking about results, profits, and cost savings that are associated with this product. Of course, the features of the product are important, but that's not what the shark wants to hear. Lead with the information she wants.

This leads me to an interesting point: the importance of eye contact. All people like to be acknowledged and there is no better way to do this than by looking someone in the eye when you talk to them. Of course, during a meeting there are lots of people to look at; most of the time you are talking to everyone. By observing the head nod, we can narrow down the number of people to look at when we talk. If, when you are making a point, you pick out the people nodding their heads and look straight at them, you will improve the effectiveness of your point. It is far easier to strengthen your point with people who like it already, than it is to turn someone's point of view around.

Making eye contact with someone who does not agree with you causes them to experience "fight or flight" syndrome. It's a confrontational stance that causes people to hang onto their opinion ever more tightly. This is the sort of thing that changes a discussion into an argument. If you cement others into your way of thinking, the people on the other side of the issue will start to change on their own. Try as often as you can to look at the head nodders.

Eyebrows Up

When someone raises one or both eyebrows, it signifies that something said surprised, disturbed, excited, or confused the person. You should watch out of this important facial gesture. Leaving someone in a state of confusion is not a good idea. If they are excited, we want to take advantage of that excitement, and if they are surprised or disturbed we what to find out why. Let's look at a quick example:

You give the price of 1.2 million for an upcoming project and Bridget, a rook, raises an eyebrow. This could mean a number of different things. It could be that Bridget thinks 1.2M is an outrageous price and the company could never afford that. Or, it could be that the last potential vendor they interviewed wanted 2.6M and your quote is so much less it was surprising. You don't know exactly what the gesture means at this point and that is not a good thing. Stop what you are saying and ask one simple question, "how does that sound?" Now, you will find out what Bridget is thinking. Once she shares her point of view, you have something to react to. If she thought the price was way too high, you can point out all the factors that caused the price. If she thought the price was way too low, you might have to convince her that you can do the complete job for that. By not allowing Bridget to speak her mind when the thought was fresh in her brain, she might write you off and you wouldn't know why.

Eyebrows Down

There are two facial gestures that mean the same thing. If someone drops both eyebrows down into a frown expression, something that was said concerned them. A gesture of similar meaning is when they push their lower lip up into their upper lip. This is sometimes called, "pursing your lips". The two gestures can be done as the same time with the same meaning. As with the eyebrow raise, it's important to discover what's on their minds right as they think it. If you allow time to go by before you ask what's up, they may have decided by that time not to tell you, or they may even have forgotten, at least for now. We don't want that to happen. A quick question us can give us the information we desire. Only this time, the question can be a lot more focused because the gesture only has one meaning. This time we can ask, "What are your concerns?" This is when people will start to think you're psychic. They have a concern and you ask what it is without even knowing they were upset. Except, secretly, you knew all along.

It's important with all of the gestures mentioned in this section to react to them quickly. If you ask questions right away, you get a truthful answer before they have a chance to think about it. Even a few seconds delay is all the time it takes for something to change their minds about sharing with you. Timing is everything.

Looking Down

The next two gestures are harder to read and take more practice, so work on the first three before you try these.

When someone looks down and to their left and their eyes start to bounce around, they are scanning their memory while trying to remember something important.

What I mean by eyes bouncing around is they don't focus on one spot. The eyes are darting back and forth. You may have heard of this concept while you're sleeping: it's known as R.E.M. (Rapid Eye Movement) and it's how doctors and scientists can tell if you're dreaming. When you dream, you are scanning your mind for memories and ideas. There is a physical connection between the eyes and the brain that causes REM. The same thing is happening here, except you're awake. So to repeat: eyes down, to the left, and rapid eye movement, all signal the expression.

While they are remembering, they have lost their focus on you. Now is not the time to attempt to tell them something important. Octopi can be doing this and still hear every word you're saying, but this is not so with the other creatures. Something that was said triggered this response and it's a good thing. They could be remembering a past experience that relates to your meeting topic. They could be trying to recall the name of someone that could help. They could be trying to remember what their spouse told them to pick up at the grocery store. You never really know if what they are thinking about relates to your meeting or not, but in many cases it will.

Most people see this gesture as being bored or losing focus on the issue at hand. They get angry that the person isn't listening to them. This is a big mistake. What do you want people to do in a meeting? THINK! We want them to think. This gesture lets you know that they are doing exactly that. Now that they are thinking, we can harvest their thoughts and everyone at the meeting can benefit. But, there is a trick to it.

The trick to getting the maximum benefit from their thought process is to let them finish thinking. You will know when they are done when they look back up at you. As soon as they do this, you need to harvest their thoughts with a simple question such as:

> *"Is there anything in your experience that relates to this?"*

> *"Have you ever dealt with this before?"*

> *"Is there anything in your history that can help us?"*

Note that all of these questions have one important element in common: they all deal with the past. They were just scanning their minds for a memory, so let's give them the chance to tell everyone what they came up with. It's amazing what you can find out if you take the opportunity to do some targeted listening.

Have you ever heard someone say, "I had something important to say, but I can't remember it now?" If this has been said to you, it's because you stepped on that person's thought process. They looked down to the left and went into R.E.M. and then when they looked up, you kept talking. By the time they had a chance to break in, they forgot what they were going to tell you. That's why it is important to always ask them what they were thinking about right when they look back at you. Stop what you are saying in mid-sentence. Yes, it's that important.

Most people really like the sound of their own voice, but as a leader you need to hear what other people are thinking. After all, you already know what you think. You need to find out what they think. This is a perfect time to do that.

You may find, while you are mining for their thoughts, that they don't want to tell you. They may say, "Oh, I wasn't thinking anything." They were thinking alright, they just weren't thinking about what was going on in the meeting. They may be scanning to remember if they fed the cat or paid the credit card bill. If this happens, do not make them feel embarrassed or stupid by pointing their lack of focus out to the group. This accomplishes nothing. Instead, just continue on with the meeting as if nothing has happened, knowing that at least you have refocused them on the topic at hand.

Looking Up

This is a very similar gesture to looking down, except the meaning is uniquely different. When a person looks up to the left and goes into R.E.M., they are dreaming up new ideas. Much of what was talked about in the last section applies here too. They are thinking hard and we want to let them finish thinking. Don't talk directly to them at this time and don't ask them a question until they look back at you. Octopi are especially prone to making this facial expression. The octopi are idea people after all, and they are always thinking up new things.

The big difference in your reaction between them looking up and looking down is the type of question you ask when they look back. Examples of the question you want to ask are:

"Do you have something you could add to this?"

"What does this make you think of?"

"How would you expand on this idea?"

Note that all these questions are about new ideas or expanding the thought process. This is not a complete list of questions, you can dream up your own, just remember to make it about the future possibilities and not about the past.

You will not be able to go into your next meeting and, POW! - be a master at this. Reading and reacting to facial gestures takes practice. I do not recommend that you practice in meetings, at least not at first. Practice with your friends, family, or in casual conversations. If you misread a cue during a non-business meeting, that's no big deal; you can blow it off and move on. Once you start to get the hang of it, then start using it in meetings to your advantage. This is probably the most time consuming technique in the book, so keep at it. It will be worth the effort.

Chapter Ten
Wrapping It All Up

At last you've come to the end of the book. You've done great, but you are not "Meeting Royalty" yet. You need to practice. Studies have proven that humans lose most of what we learn in the first 24 hours after we hear it. The techniques in this book will take some time and effort to cement in your head.

I want to leave you with a work schedule to help turn you into a meeting master. You've taken the first and biggest step, but now let's go the rest of the way. The next thing to do is take the quiz at the end of this chapter to see if you've understood the key points. You can write in the book if you want, but I suggest writing your answers on a separate piece of paper so you can take the test again in the future.

Once you've taken the quiz and have checked your answers, the next thing you want to do is pick one technique and start applying it. You can identify chess pieces, notice people's game strategy, guess what sea creature they are, or read facial gestures. Trying to do all four at once would probably be overwhelming. Practice until you start feeling comfortable with one technique, then switch to the next. You can integrate the two techniques after you have the second one working. Continue the process until you have working knowledge of all four techniques.

After two weeks of practice, read this book again. You will be surprised at how much you missed the first time around. After the third reading, do not throw the book away or give it to a friend. Instead, put the book back on the shelf to use for future reference. You may never need it again, but a reminder once in awhile is never a bad idea.

Quiz Begins On Next Page

The Quiz

(the answer key is at the end)

Rating: Give yourself one point for every answer you get correct.

25-30 - You're on your way to becoming "Meeting Royalty"!

20-25 - You're not the King or the Queen, but you might be a Knight.

15-20 - Time to read the book again.

<15 - Send in the Pawns!!!

Part 1: Rate the following statements as *True* or *False*.

1) A Rook has a lot of influence in a company.

2) While trying to disarm a Knight, you should directly attack their credibility.

3) Always share a smile with a Dolphin.

4) The best time to make a reaction tree is before the meeting.

5) On a meeting diagram, KnD is not the same as Dkn.

6) There are six motivational factors to track in a meeting.

7) Someone who has authority and influence is a good candidate for a Queen.

8) The most important thing to a Crab is ideas.

9) Raising one eyebrow means something different from raising both eyebrows.

10) In a meeting, always present your most important ideas first.

11) Sharks hate to waste time.

12) BO stands for Bishop/Octopus.

13) You should always protect pawns in a meeting.

14) A Knight is good at triangulating.

15) A great job for an Octopus would be coming up with theme for the next corporate event.

Part 2 On Next Page

Part Two: Pick the best possible answer answer to each of the questions below. (multiple choice)

16) If you lose the King, you lose:

    a) Influence
    b) Authority
    c) The game
    d) Your car keys

17) A Dolphin's primary motivational factor is:

    a) Relationships
    b) Processes
    c) Money
    d) Fish
    e) None of the above

18) A clique is different from an alliance because:

    a) Cliques are only men
    b) Cliques back each other up no matter what
    c) Cliques are short term alliances
    d) Cliques contain only pawns
    e) None of the above

19) Looking down and to the left means:

    a) Nothing without R.E.M.
    b) The person is thinking up new ideas.
    c) There's a spider on the ground.
    d) The person doesn't like what you said.
    e) None of the above

20) On a meeting diagram, you should:

    a) Connect loose alliances with a dotted line.
    b) Track cliques on the outside of the table.
    c) Identify every person by where they are sitting.
    d) All of the above.
    e) None of the above.

21) RC stands for:

    a) Rook/C.E.O.
    b) Rook/Connector
    c) Rook/Champion
    d) None of the above.

22) A head nod means:

    a) I'm interested
    b) I agree with you
    c) A or B
    d) A and B

23) An Octopus' favorite color is:

    a) Red
    b) Blue
    c) Green
    d) Gray
    e) This is a trick question

24) The two motivational types who have the hardest time getting along are:

> a) Sharks and Crabs
> b) Sharks and Dolphins
> c) Octopi and Dolphins
> d) Crabs and Octopi
> e) B and D
> f) A and C
> g) None of them get along

25) Which statement would a Dolphin hate the most?

> a) Everyone has to agree.
> b) That's not my job.
> c) We need more money.
> d) I want to you work alone on this one.

26) On a decision tree, how many levels should you include?

> a) Two
> b) Three
> c) As many as you can until you fill up the paper.
> d) As many as possible.

27) Kings always:

> a) Sit at the head of the table.
> b) Wear a suit.
> c) Are usually Sharks.
> d) None of the above.

28) The best way to change the mind of an obstinate Queen is to:

    a) Fire them.
    b) Put everything in writing.
    c) Find Bishops they trust and get them to talk.
    d) Talk to the King.

29) The best type of King is:

    a) An internal one.
    b) An external one.
    c) One who switches between internal and external.
    d) None of the above.

30) An octopus is:

    a) Thought to have been born that way.
    b) A loner.
    c) Makes up 20% of the population.
    d) A and C.
    e) B and C.

Answer Key On Next Page

1 - F (Rooks have authority, not influence)

2 - F (You attack the allies of the knight)

3 - T, 4 - T, 5 - F

6 - F (There are four: Sharks, Dolphins, Octopi, and Crabs)

7 - T

8 - F (The most important things to a Crab are processes)

9 - F (The two gestures mean the same thing)

10 - F, 11 - T, 12 - T, 13 - F, 14 - T, 15 - T

16 - C, 17 - A, 18 - B, 19 - A, 20 - D, 21 - D, 22 - C

23 - E, 24 - E, 25 - D, 26 - D, 27 - D, 28 - C,

29 - C, 30 - A

Who is Cliff Suttle

Cliff Suttle is a sought after business speaker and lecturer. He is known for not only educating the audience, but delighting them at the same time. Realizing that he had a gift and a passion for business communications, Mr. Suttle founded and became the president of ExciteYourAudience.com a company dedicated to world class business/audience communications. This company not only supplies top of the game speaking talent for business events, but also teaches others how to be master communicators, convey their message and make it stick by hosting events that increase the company's bottom line.

Mr. Suttle is an awarding winning speaker, with over eighty championship titles to his credit. He is the creator of the six-CD set, "Audience in the Palm - Speech Coach in a Box," which coaches people on different aspects of public speaking. He is the author of wildly popular book "The Anti-Elevator Speech." Mr. Suttle is a successful freelance writer for print and multimedia publications and has been read internationally by millions.

Mr. Suttle gained over twenty years of solid executive business experience as CEO of a custom software consulting firm, which supplied major software solutions for small businesses to Fortune 500 companies including General Motors, Ford Motor, IBM, Blue Cross/Blue Shield, Kodak, Xerox, Metlife, Rockwell International and many more. Besides the usual CEO duties, Mr. Suttle was also the visual component for the company making presentations to business audiences from board of director meetings to large public events with thousands of attendees.

Mr. Suttle earned his B.S. in Management Information Sciences from the University of Michigan and is a certified Perk Performance Consultant.

ExciteYourAudience.com

Want to excite your audience? These products and services will help you do exactly that.

Hired Gun Speakers (Need a Speaker?)

Corporate Presentations
Corporate Sponsored Events
Marketing Events
Fund Raisers
Promotional Events

Presentation Coaching

Speech Writing
Delivery Coaching
Public Speaking Skills Training

Workshop and Keynotes

Presentation Skills, Motivational/Inspirational, Networking, Sales Skills, Team Building, Customer Service, Business Communications Skills, others customized to your organization's needs.

Products

Books, CD's, and DVD's on a variety of topics

Contact Us Today, and Excite Your Next Audience! **www.ExciteYourAudience.com**